First World War
and Army of Occupation
War Diary
France, Belgium and Germany

3 INDIAN (LAHORE) DIVISION
Divisional Troops
Royal Army Medical Corps
8 British Field Ambulance
11 August 1914 - 30 November 1915

WO95/3920/2

The Naval & Military Press Ltd
www.nmarchive.com
Published in association with The National Archives

Published by

The Naval & Military Press Ltd

Unit 10 Ridgewood Industrial Park,

Uckfield, East Sussex,

TN22 5QE England

Tel: +44 (0) 1825 749494

www.naval-military-press.com

www.nmarchive.com

This diary has been reprinted in facsimile from the original. Any imperfections are inevitably reproduced and the quality may fall short of modern type and cartographic standards.

© **Crown Copyright**
Images reproduced by permission of The National Archives, London, England, 2015.

Contents

Document type	Place/Title	Date From	Date To
Heading	WO95/3920/2		
Heading	BEF 3 Ind Lahore Div Troops No 8 British Fld Amb 1914 Aug-1915 Nov		
Heading	War Diary of Lt. Col. T. Duts Whaite R.A.M.C. O.C. No 8 British Fd Ambce Lahore Division From 11th Aug 1914 To 31st October 1914 Vol I		
War Diary	Lahore Cant	11/08/1914	15/08/1914
War Diary	Reti	16/08/1914	16/08/1914
War Diary	Karachi	17/08/1914	29/08/1914
War Diary	At Sea	30/08/1914	05/09/1914
War Diary	Aden	06/09/1914	07/09/1914
War Diary	At Sea	08/09/1914	13/09/1914
War Diary	Suez	14/09/1914	16/09/1914
War Diary	Alexandria	17/09/1914	19/09/1914
War Diary	At Sea	20/09/1914	25/09/1914
War Diary	Marseilles	26/09/1914	30/09/1914
War Diary	On Train	01/10/1914	02/10/1914
War Diary	Orleans	03/10/1914	18/10/1914
War Diary	With Train	19/10/1914	19/10/1914
War Diary	Lumbres	20/10/1914	20/10/1914
War Diary	Arques	21/10/1914	21/10/1914
War Diary	Hazebrouck	22/10/1914	23/10/1914
War Diary	Estaires For Le Drumez	24/10/1914	24/10/1914
War Diary	La Casan	24/10/1914	24/10/1914
War Diary	Nr Locon	24/10/1914	25/10/1914
War Diary	La Casan	25/10/1914	26/10/1914
War Diary	La Gorgue	27/10/1914	27/10/1914
War Diary	Lame Blau	28/10/1914	28/10/1914
War Diary	La Gorgue	29/10/1914	31/10/1914
Heading	War Diary Of The Officer Commanding No 8 British Field Ambulance Lahore Division D.E. Force Forth Month of November 1914		
War Diary	Lagorgue Nr Estaires	01/11/1914	16/11/1914
War Diary	Locon	17/11/1914	22/11/1914
War Diary	Chateau Gorre	23/11/1914	24/11/1914
War Diary	Les, Choquiaux	25/11/1914	01/12/1914
War Diary	Hingette	03/12/1914	12/12/1914
War Diary	Chau-Gorre	13/12/1914	14/12/1914
War Diary	Beuvry	15/12/1914	22/12/1914
War Diary	Allouagne	23/12/1914	31/12/1914
Miscellaneous	Messages And Signals	01/12/1914	01/12/1914
Miscellaneous	Messages And Signals	03/12/1914	03/12/1914
Miscellaneous	Messages And Signals	11/12/1914	11/12/1914
Miscellaneous	Messages And Signals	13/12/1914	13/12/1914
Miscellaneous	Messages And Signals	15/12/1914	15/12/1914
Miscellaneous	Messages And Signals	17/12/1914	17/12/1914
Miscellaneous	Messages And Signals	18/12/1914	18/12/1914
Miscellaneous	Messages And Signals	19/12/1914	19/12/1914
Miscellaneous	Messages And Signals	20/12/1914	20/12/1914
Miscellaneous	Messages And Signals	21/12/1914	21/12/1914

Type	Description	Start	End
Miscellaneous	Messages And Signals	22/12/1914	22/12/1914
Miscellaneous	Messages And Signals	23/12/1914	23/12/1914
Heading	War Diary of No 8 British Field Ambulance From 1st January 1915 To, 31st January 1915		
War Diary	Allouagne	01/01/1915	31/01/1915
Miscellaneous	Messages And Signals	25/01/1915	25/01/1915
Operation(al) Order(s)	Operation Order No. 35 by Colonel B.B. Grayfoot A.D.M.S. Lahore Divn	25/01/1915	25/01/1915
Miscellaneous	Messages And Signals	25/01/1915	25/01/1915
Miscellaneous	Messages And Signals	26/01/1915	26/01/1915
Miscellaneous	Messages And Signals	27/01/1915	27/01/1915
Operation(al) Order(s)	Operation Order No. 48 by Colonel B.B. Grayfoot A.D.M.S. Lahore Divn	29/01/1915	29/01/1915
Heading	War Diary of With Appendices No. 8 British Field Ambulance From 1st February 1915 To 28th February 1915		
Miscellaneous	Messages And Signals. App-I		
Miscellaneous	A Form. Messages And Signals. App II	20/02/1915	20/02/1915
Miscellaneous	A Form. Messages And Signals. App III	22/02/1915	22/02/1915
Miscellaneous	App IV	22/02/1915	22/02/1915
War Diary	Allouagne To St Floris	01/02/1915	01/02/1915
War Diary	St. Floris	02/02/1915	09/02/1915
War Diary	St. Floris To Locon	10/02/1915	10/02/1915
War Diary	Locon	11/02/1915	22/02/1915
War Diary	Locon To St. Floris	23/02/1915	23/02/1915
War Diary	St. Floris	24/02/1915	28/02/1915
Heading	War Diary of with Appendices No 8 British Field Ambulance; Lahore Division From 1st March 1915 To, 31st March 1915		
War Diary	War Diary Of Officer Commanding No 8 British Field Ambulance Lahore Division For Month of March 1915		
War Diary	St. Floris	01/03/1915	10/03/1915
War Diary	St. Floris To Le Cornet Malo	10/03/1915	12/03/1915
War Diary	Vieille Chapelle	13/03/1915	24/03/1915
War Diary	Calonne	25/03/1915	31/03/1915
Miscellaneous	A Form. Messages And Signals. App I		
Miscellaneous	B Form. Messages And Signals. App II		
Miscellaneous	A Form. Messages And Signals. Appendix III		
Miscellaneous	B Form. Messages And Signals. App IV		
Miscellaneous	A Form. Messages And Signals. Appendix V		
Miscellaneous	A Form. Messages And Signals. Appendix VI		
War Diary	Calonne	01/04/1915	24/04/1915
War Diary	Ouderdom	25/04/1915	25/04/1915
War Diary	Vlamertinghe	26/04/1915	27/04/1915
War Diary	Ouderdom Road	27/04/1915	29/04/1915
War Diary	Renninghelst	30/04/1915	30/04/1915
Miscellaneous	Copy of a letter from G.D M.S G.H.Q No. P937	05/04/1915	05/04/1915
Miscellaneous	App. III	05/04/1915	05/04/1915
Miscellaneous	Oc No.8 B F H Calonne		
Miscellaneous	Field Ambulance		
Miscellaneous	Oc No.8 B F A		
Miscellaneous	Field Ambulance		
Miscellaneous	Oc No. 8 B F A		
Miscellaneous	O.C. No 8 B.F.A Oderdum		
Miscellaneous	O.C. No. 8 B.F.A		
War Diary	Renninghelst Boeschepe	01/05/1915	01/05/1915

War Diary	Boeschepe	02/05/1915	02/05/1915
War Diary	Calonne	03/05/1915	06/05/1915
War Diary	R.16.e (Map 'France' 1/40,000, Bethune.)	04/05/1915	31/05/1915
Miscellaneous	No. 8 B F.A.		
Miscellaneous	O.C. 8. B.F.A. Appendix I	01/05/1915	01/05/1915
Miscellaneous	O.C. 8. B.F.A. Appendix II	01/05/1915	01/05/1915
Miscellaneous	O.C. 8. B.F.A. Appendix III	02/05/1915	02/05/1915
Miscellaneous	O.C. 8. B.F.A. Appendix IV	06/05/1915	06/05/1915
Miscellaneous	O.C. 8. B.F.A. Appendix V	07/05/1915	07/05/1915
Miscellaneous	Copy Order from A.D.M.S. Lahore Division. Appendix VI	08/05/1915	08/05/1915
Miscellaneous	O.C. 8. B.F.A. Appendix VII	08/05/1915	08/05/1915
Miscellaneous	O.C. 8. B.F.A. Appendix VIII	11/05/1915	11/05/1915
Miscellaneous	O.C. 8. B.F.A. Appendix IX	11/05/1915	11/05/1915
Miscellaneous	O.C. 8. B.F.A. Appendix X	15/05/1915	15/05/1915
Miscellaneous	To Lieut Warwick R.A.M.C. 8. B.F.A. Appendix XI	15/05/1915	15/05/1915
Miscellaneous	O.C. 8. B.F.A. Appendix XII	16/05/1915	16/05/1915
Miscellaneous	O.C. 8. B.F.A. R.16.C Appendix XIII	18/05/1915	18/05/1915
Miscellaneous	O.C. Bearer Division. Appendix XIV	18/05/1915	18/05/1915
Miscellaneous	No 8. B.F.A. R.16.C. Appendix XV	18/05/1915	18/05/1915
Miscellaneous	8. B.F.A. Appendix XVI	18/05/1915	18/05/1915
Miscellaneous	8. B.F.A. R.16.C. Appendix XVII	18/05/1915	18/05/1915
Miscellaneous	O.C. No. 8. B.F.A. Appendix XVIII	20/05/1915	20/05/1915
Miscellaneous	Departmental Order by Colonel B.B. Grayfoot C.M.S. A.D.M.S. Lahore Division. Appendix XIX		
Miscellaneous	Copy of No D.D. 184 6/7 dated 24.5.15. from the A.D.M.S. Indian Corps. Appendix XX	24/05/1915	24/05/1915
Miscellaneous	Extract from Field Ambulance Order by Major A.W. Gibson R.A.M.C. Comndg no 8. B.F.A. Appendix XXI	25/05/1915	25/05/1915
Miscellaneous	No 8. B.F.A. Appendix XXII	25/05/1915	25/05/1915
Miscellaneous	O.C. No 8. B.F.A. Appendix XXIII	28/05/1915	28/05/1915
Miscellaneous	Deptt Order by Col. B.B. Grayfoot C.M.S. A.D.M.S. Lahore Division of 28.5.15. Appendix XXIV	28/05/1915	28/05/1915
Miscellaneous	No 8. B.F.A. Appendix XXV	30/05/1915	30/05/1915
Miscellaneous	D.A.G 3rd Echelon	04/07/1915	04/07/1915
War Diary	R.16.C	01/06/1915	30/06/1915
Heading	War Diary of No 8 British Field Ambulance-Lahore Divn From 1st July 1915 To 31st July 1915		
War Diary	R. 16.C	01/07/1915	15/07/1915
Map	Map		
War Diary	The Patronage La. Gorgue	15/07/1915	31/07/1915
Heading	War Diary of No 8 Field Ambulance From 1st August 1915 To 31st August 1915		
War Diary	'Pahonage' La Gorgue	01/08/1915	02/08/1915
War Diary	Vieille Chapelle	03/08/1915	31/08/1915
Heading	War Diary of No 8 British Field Ambulance From 1st September 1915 To 30th September 1915		
War Diary	Vielle Chapelle	01/09/1915	30/09/1915
Heading	War Diary of No 8 British Field Ambulance From 1st October 1915 To 31st October 1915		
War Diary	Vielle Chapelle	01/10/1915	18/10/1915
War Diary	L'Epinette	19/10/1915	31/10/1915
Heading	War Diary of No 8 British Field Ambulance Lahore Division From 1st November 1915 To 30th November 1915		
War Diary	L'Epinette	01/11/1915	08/11/1915

War Diary	Fontes	08/11/1915	18/11/1915
War Diary	Witternesse	18/11/1915	29/11/1915
War Diary	Enquin	29/11/1915	30/11/1915

BEF

3 IND. LAHORE DIV TROOPS

NO 8 BRITISH FLD AMB

1914 AUG — 1915 NOV

TO MESOPOTAMIA

Army Form C. 2118.

WAR DIARY
or
INTELLIGENCE SUMMARY.

(Erase heading not required.)

Confidential
War Diary
of
Lt. Col. J. Duke Wharton Rawie.
O.C. No 8 British Field Amb.
Lahore Division.
31st October

From 11th Aug 1914 to 29th Septr 1914.
(Vol. II.)

WAR DIARY or **INTELLIGENCE SUMMARY**

Army Form C. 2118.

U. Col. Whaite RAMC
O.C. No. 8. British F.A. Sub.
Lahore Divn.

(1)

Instructions regarding War Diaries and Intelligence Summaries are contained in F. S. Regs., Part II, and the Staff Manual respectively. Title pages will be prepared in manuscript.

(Erase heading not required.)

Hour, Date, Place.	Summary of Events and Information.	Remarks and references to Appendices.
8 am 11th Aug 1914 LAHORE CANTT.	Mobilization of No. 8 British Field Ambulance commenced at Mob'n Stores 3rd LAHORE DIVN. — The old schedule has been superseded by a new one for which we received memorandum copy. All differences in packages are being filled up and new designation stencilled on boxes +c.	70/1
10 am 14 Aug '14 — do —	Mobilization being completed apace fourth, we took out personnel to the Parade Ground of 26th P.I. Deptt. At 7 p.m. we were inspected by the A.D.M.S. 3rd LAHORE DIVN. Personnel as follows. LT.COL. T. DUB. WHAITE R.A.M.S. in command of unit. — I.S.M.D. — Major A.W. GIBSON R.A.M.C. "A" Set'n ["A" Sec. Add Sgn. 16th Cl. E.O. JOHNSON Capt. R.J. FRANKLIN — do — "B" " " " 4th " H.B. BLAKER. Lieut. J.W. LANE — do — "D" Lieut. × BRUCE — do — "C" "B" Set'n. 3rd Clan Asst Surg 2nd R.H.S. GILLESPIE and A.G. FRASER "C" " " " " " B.J. BOUCHÉ. "D" " " " " " H. FOX. " " " " " " G.R. FIDO " " " " " " A.W. CUMMINS. 4 Pakistani Sergeants. 8 Nursing Orderlies & 10 Bahmen. – I.S.t. Engt. 50 Army Hospital Corps and 133 Army/Bearer Corps – 3 Horses – 2 Hospital Stretchers. – 2 Asst ditto. 4 Pakeali Bhisties, & 2 Tailors. –	× Relieved by Major H.F. SHEA at KARACHI. 20.8.'14. 70/1
8.30 am 15th Aug. '14. LAHORE CANTT.	Entrainment at Rest Camp siding. Moved off at about 10.45 am. at KHANEWAL Jn an extra 3rd Clan Bogie Carriage was put on as the men were very overcrowded the heat great. A.B.C. Capted Brunials Shopkeeper and were most troublesome. They were warned it should not recur again.	70/1
16 Aug. '14. RET.	Same occurred again. At Rohri paraded all in platform and again warned them. Told them any claims against would be a general charge against all the & Ambulance on the Train.	70/1

Army Form C. 2118.

WAR DIARY
or
INTELLIGENCE SUMMARY.
(Erase heading not required.)

Hour, Date, Place.	Summary of Events and Information.	Remarks and references to Appendices.
9.45 A.M. 17th Aug. KARACHI.	Arrived at Rest Camp and detrained - Standing Camp. All ricks to be seen and treated by individual Units: men receiving admission tickets will be taken away by a tonga at 9am sharp - have arrangements for Billets and instruction B.A.B.C. whilst in Camp here -	Drew SSD/- advance for men & British Personnel vide accounts MW
18th Aug '14. KARACHI.	Camp routine. Quarting Brassards & Identity Discs for A.B.C. are indented for. Boots but neither looks nor shoes as he had.	Drew Rs 165/- for Asst Sgts turning over Vels. Rs 175/-[?] (vide account) MW
19th Aug '14. — do —	Under instruction from A.D.M.S. KARACHI. 1 B.D.E. ordered 133 Divs for A.B.C. HERMAN + Co. Majority of Wheels issued to all A.B.C. (not already in possession of them) - Sophing actg Quinin & I issued to all daily.	MW
20th Aug '14. do.	Major H.F.SHEA R.A.M.C. joined and Lt BRUCE returned to his station. Received 20 stretchers and 133 Divs for A.B.C - Saddles for Asst Sgts will be issued at Base.	MW
21st Aug. '14. do.	Routine as above - Major SHEA's horse arrived -	MW
22nd Aug '14. do -	Nothing special to note - No 2 Mule Corps will supply from 8 Draught Mules	MW
23rd Aug. 14. do	Sent Copies of our Standing order for No 6 B.F.A to A.Dms. 3rd Indn Div.	MW
24th Aug. 14. do.	A.D.M.S. + R.A.D.M.S.(Indn) left today to embark in S.S. Glasgow (C.i/c of) A.D.M.S. Karachi B.D.E will carry on - and I am sending everything all Documents to his referring to him	MW
25 Aug. 14. — do —	Received List of Brassards. (Said to be incorrect in some way: but same cannot get our stores.) Issued 195 to No 112.9. F.A - 85 to DC No7 B.F.A 2 to Asst of 2 Mandulay R. and Kept 250 ourselves - and returned the balance about 900 to A.Dms. Karachi BDE	Drew Rs. 123 of- advance of pay for 2 Asst Sgts from 410 Bearer (vide account.)

P.T.O.

Army Form C. 2118.

WAR DIARY
or
INTELLIGENCE SUMMARY.

(Erase heading not required.)

3

Hour, Date, Place.	Summary of Events and Information.	Remarks and references to Appendices.
25th Aug. '14. KARACHI.	Warned verbally by A.Q.M.G. Br.: Bde to be ready for an early order to embark. Section of Potaties leave presented two cases of contagion. Fearing some further trouble, the other Cipaithi tea sources for patients. Wrote to thank them.	MW
26th Aug. 14. do.	Ordered to be in readiness to embark at short notice — no order came —	MW
27th Aug. 14. do.	Again ordered to be ready to embark at very short notice. An Intim. after noon late in afternoon received information we were not to embark today — The men and our officers had been standing by practically since yesterday — Asked if new train or march to Kiamari — Chose train —	MW
28th Aug. 14. do.	Troop train arrived at 1 p.m. Drew our 8 mules. Tom. No 2 mule Cart, and rode myself with transport animals and 2 chargers of 2 British & 3 Indian 3 Chambers to KIMARI. When I embarked the mules in transport "ITAURA" & the horses in the H.T. "Castalia". The embarkation of the mules was very slow, and it was after midnight when all were onboard. The embarkation Staff were not what one would call affable and except two from hospital. Received instructions to make one consignment up to 25 per 25 cub.ft. 250 Sheep coming on board for rations of British Personnel, Ourselves & 32 Sig. Signal Co. Supper Ammn. The only place for a hospital is the Smoking Room!! This ship is 1st class only and there is very little accommodation from ladies. A proposal by sleep Doctor at Bombay where this voyage began was to have two temporary hospitals on promenade deck. This was negatived as impracticable. Looking	MW

WAR DIARY
or
INTELLIGENCE SUMMARY.

Army Form C. 2118.

(Erase heading not required.)

Hour, Date, Place.	Summary of Events and Information.	Remarks and references to Appendices.
29th Aug. KARACHI.	Left port at 1.30 p.m. and soon after accompanied O.C. Troops. Lt.Col. C.COFFIN. R.E. round the ship — and did all we could to make the men comfortable. Our Convoy consists of 7 been Transports escorted by H.M.S. "NORTHBROOK." Men made outside hammocks. Many natives sick.	Run.
30th Aug. At Sea.	Sunday. Church Service 11 a.m. Swell at sea — vessel pitching —	Run 137 miles —
1st Sept. —do—	Fairly strong head wind, pitching. Acting Lieut. on "SANGOLA" reports case of partially strangled hernia — a surgeon. There is no med. officer in the ship and no ship's surgeon — too rough to transfer self from this ship — Weather rock travel —	Run 17 181 "
2 Sept. —do—	Still too rough to put out a boat. Men report that much the same. All natives throw up on deck and refuse to be unrolled out —	" 168 "
3rd Sept. —do—	Major GIBSON. Transferred to "SANGOLA" and operated to relieve the hernia. The General) We are having a series of conferences on first or sanitation. Life belts fitted and all men exercised on deck from 8-10 p.m.	" 181 "
4 Sept. —do—	Routine of Board ship life —	" 164 "
5 Sept. —do—	ditto — H.M.S. "CHATHAM" joined us —	" 212 "
6 Sept. ADEN.	Arrived at Aden 4 p.m. Major GIBSON rejoined ship a ryt. the man has had three of the limps. recommends landing him here —	" 200 "

Army Form C. 2118.

5

WAR DIARY
or
INTELLIGENCE SUMMARY.

(Erase heading not required.)

Instructions regarding War Diaries and Intelligence Summaries are contained in F. S. Regs., Part II, and the Staff Manual respectively. Title pages will be prepared in manuscript.

Hour, Date, Place.	Summary of Events and Information.	Remarks and references to Appendices.
7th Sept '14. ADEN.	Horse exercise and stills round out and lines; no leave of flies found but flies very numerous — Med. Officer of Port tells me the man with Hernia and tubercle died in his hosp. at 3am today — Sailed about 8.30 p.m.	Run 136 miles. OWN
8th Sept. At Sea.	Head wind — remarkably cool. Had part of awning removed from troop deck in the hold under it — men very stuffy there feeling heat.	" 229 " OWN
9th Sept. —do—	Still cool. Sail with rigged in No 2 hold for natives — Started a French class for subordinates — Nalin has a peculiar bitter alcoholic taste attributed to experimenting of tanks — New tank taken into use which tastes all right —	" 217 " OWN
10th Sept. —do—	Still cool. Ship's Doctor asked me to see Captain Mitchell of the Ship. I found him ill with fever and Sunday symptoms 101.2° objects to 7am in his cabin & keeps ports closed —	" 202 " OWN
11th Sept. —do—	The poor old Captain died in the night, his Certificate at 7am being 105 under Tongue points to Head stroke — Funeral at 10 a.m.	" 222 " OWN
12 Sept. —do—	Still cool headwind. Boars Tmn S. "BLACK PRINCE" ontward bound. Captain Walsh's (Conn Ranger) horse died of heat stroke — Concert in music Room —	" 218 " OWN

WAR DIARY or INTELLIGENCE SUMMARY.

Army Form C. 2118.

(Erase heading not required.)

Hour, Date, Place.	Summary of Events and Information.	Remarks and references to Appendices.
13th Sept. 1914. Sunday.	Church Service 10.30 a.m. Mine laying suspected (by a Dhow) Precautions taken. Arrived Suez at sundown and anchored for the night.	
14th Sept. '14. SUEZ.	Moved to wharf. 32nd Signal Co. disembarked will be railed to Cairo. We remain on board and go round to Alexandria. Three privates left ship and one returned drunk - 135th (recovered absent) ie. Pte Clisto.	
15th Sept. '14	Suez to Port Said - arrived 8 p.m. coaling all night.	
16th Sept. '14	Left Port Said at 6 a.m. arr. Alexandria at 9 p.m. anchored.	
17th Sept. '14. ALEXANDRIA.	Moved into dock in forenoon. Men taken for a walk on shore: they are quite fit - having been exercised regularly every day. Mules & several horses slung on shore and their places in ship thoroughly cleaned out.	
18th Sept. -do.-	Stretchers got out and men exercised with them. C.O.'s & Glasgow into staff in pith helmets to town. Handed over 3 pil. cases to the A.D.M.S. also some Typhoid Vaccine. All other transport are re-embarking their troops.	

Army Form C. 2118.

WAR DIARY
or
INTELLIGENCE SUMMARY.
(Erase heading not required.)

Instructions regarding War Diaries and Intelligence Summaries are contained in F. S. Regs., Part II, and the Staff Manual respectively. Title pages will be prepared in manuscript.

Hour, Date, Place.	Summary of Events and Information.	Remarks and references to Appendices.
19th Sept. 14.	Left Alexandria at 12 noon. Suffield "DEVANA" with Army and Naval material from my Division the Colonial train. Artillery inoculations, 2nd Dose. 16 vessels in our Convoy, escorted by H.M.S. "WEYMOUTH" at sundown met ships of Port Said Convoy, 6 in number.	Manchester & Com. Rogers. JW
20th Sept. 14. Sunday. at Sea.	H.M.S. "INDOMITABLE" joins us. Church Parade 10.30 a.m.	Run 198 miles — JW
21 Sept. 14. At Sea.	Kit-inspection. Greatcoats & Jerseys made list of deficiencies for replacement at Base. H.M.S. Indom: left us today.	" 216 " JW
22 Sept. 14. — do —	Met fleet of 12 Transports convoyed by H.M.S. "MINERVA" for Territorials for Egypt — we exchange convoy eastwards — exchanged escorts —	" 215 " JW
23rd Sept.14. — do —	Nothing Special	" 188 " JW
24th Sept.14. — do —	Made a several plate (No 8) and stamped all braces — also signed them with (13FA) aniline pencil over office stamp —	" 220 " to Marseilles JW
25 Sept. 14. — do —	Made out return of kits on board and settled who should be transferred sick when we arrive.	JW

WAR DIARY

INTELLIGENCE SUMMARY.

(Erase heading not required.)

Army Form C. 2118.

Instructions regarding War Diaries and Intelligence Summaries are contained in F.S. Regs., Part II, and the Staff Manual respectively. Title pages will be prepared in manuscript.

Hour, Date, Place.	Summary of Events and Information.	Remarks and references to Appendices.
6 a.m. 26 Sept '14. Marseilles	Came alongside 10 a.m. to unload. Sent off two lorries with Rits+ return under W.O.s & gun to Parc Borely, with [party of] personnel & baresleit. After 2 calls more returns until 6 p.m. and plenty of carload were still in the Shed. This we left under a guard till tomorrow morning. We reached Camp at about 8 p.m. The Advance is about 5 mile. Lt Col COFFIN, C.- R.E. & Capt. LANE, R.A.M.C. Tienp.d. rick 5th Anglo French R. with fever. 2 British (Venereal) & 6 natives (prison) taken over by No 7 B.F.A. refer divin at Chateau de L'EVÊQUE. Major SHEA Conp. NO 7 B.F.A. as Surgical Specialist and Lieut BIGGAM, locked to me from No 7 B.F.A. Re-departure. Lahore Div.= machine gun mules, latines & in Camp.	9 m
27. Sept. '14 MARSEILLES	With early morning camp, and superintending sterilization of the mule with Alum. + Calc. Chlor. The life Suffle is from Canal and not safe to drinking. Lanterns posted and Reft. Med. Officer Floating Refs. Near w instructed in press and advised as to there to. Latrine shot-trench about 18" deep dug in ridden space set apart for them.	W
28 Sept. 1914. -do-	Arranged Reserve Division in accordance with Adjue's instructions. Route march. Bathing Parade and Shelter side for men. Mistral sprang up in the night and some tent poles broke. (Inconvenient.)	W
29th Sept '14 -do-	Storm with much dust. blowing all day. Insp. & instructor for ver. More formed. Order received for entrainment tomorrow. Visited French. Mil. Hospt. with Major BROWN & GIBSON. very cordial.	W

Army Form C. 2118.

WAR DIARY
or
INTELLIGENCE SUMMARY.

(Erase heading not required.)

Hour, Date, Place.	Summary of Events and Information.	Remarks and references to Appendices.
1.30 P.M. 30 Sep. Marseilles.	Struck camp. Baggage & personnel moved off for No 2 Platform Gare d'Arenq. Train left at 8.25 p.m.	
1st Oct. – on Train – Oct. 1/14.	Route via Cette, NARBONNE, MONTAUBAN, TOULOUSE, CAHORS, LIMOGES ST. SULPICE LAURIERE to LES AUBRAIS (ORLEANS) Halts at stated intervals for cooking food, latrines and ablutions – Guards posted in front and rear brake vans to prevent men from leaving train – Passed thru' wine districts – were given plenty of grapes.	
2nd Oct.'14.	Early halt at LIMOGES (Feuillets) & at St SULPICE LAURIERE (Halte Repas) about 11 a.m. for 4 hours. Passed thro' fruit districts during day and arrived at LES AUBRAIS (ORLEANS) about midnight.	
3rd Oct 14. 2.A.M. ORLEANS –	Having loaded up the Ambulance large wagons we marched & tramped and got them about 4 a.m. pitched a few tents and turned in until daylight. Received orders from D.D.M.S. to open for reception of British sick – Had Tenlans on ground to do so. Tents that allotted to No 7 B.F.A. even then were granted to Room & Latrines are Flanders in Needs M. & Capt across the road – Does for trate Cats. which are Pole pattern. 2 Nurses – Water good but suffer civilian industrial neighbourhood. Drew 6 Amb. & wagon complete –	
4th Oct 14. ditto –	Genl. Willcocks visited Camp with Staff. He gave orders for cars. Red crossed to be made for both sides of each tent. Am fitting up all permits from the ambulance linen. Built incinerator. Edge up for litter &c.	
5th Oct.'14. ditto.	Replied to No 5379 (ADMS) copy of memo No 1-IG dated 7. Sep.14. from G.S. & ADMS. re languages &c. 1. Lt Col. WHITE v.g. French & German. Major GIBSON. Capt FRANKLIN fair colloquial French Lt BIGG.R.M. " " German.	

John Willcocks

over –

Army Form C. 2118.

WAR DIARY
INTELLIGENCE SUMMARY.
(Erase heading not required.)

Instructions regarding War Diaries and Intelligence Summaries are contained in F.S. Regs., Part II, and the Staff Manual respectively. Title pages will be prepared in manuscript.

Hour, Date, Place.	Summary of Events and Information.	Remarks and references to Appendices.
5th Oct. '14. Orleans. (Cont'd)	2) All Officers trained in map reading & for Col WHITE is a good panorama sketcher. N.C.O's also Regimentally in topography & panorama sketching. Transport Sergt BROWNING & 8 Hussars - also reconnaissance. 3) There have been two Intelligence Courses - Next to O.D ran Depot at LA CHAPELLE & Drew warm underclothing for nature.	
6th Oct. '14. Orleans.	Held ward & orderly Officer Changes - Lt Col WHITE's & SD Maj GIBSON's at 8.45. Ridley Jones & standing in for Asst Surg & Transport Sergt. The latter is certainly a Smart minister as Conmst efficiently supervise transport of all students for camp outfits £1 8150 drawing to sufficient normal viands and leftover some issued to Units -	
7th Oct '14 Orleans.	Censor stamp received with orders for its use - Censor correspondence. Army personal and patients in hospital - Acknowledge Receipt of same - Wrote letter to Treas: India - re Grant of Rupees 1500 for confederates the maintenance of Efficiency of this Unit - Calculated Rate of pay & as begins by B:170 Amb. = B:0 300 and for the Bearer Division = B:0 100 - 10 Uneemaled cars trans: to No 10 Stationary Hospt. in ORLEANS.	
8th Oct '14 Orleans.	Daily state to show casualties of A.M.C. & A.B.C. separately - so as to facilitate replacement.	
9th Oct '14 Orleans.	On Parade are not stamped by Govt of India and these are normal Official nos available. Took over - 4 Baggage wagons, 1 Supply wagon & 1 Cooks wagon all Horsed. The Cooks wagon is really a sort of ration (more or less) apparatus.) Received Outfits of Official books - and issues them to the Field Ambulances	Senior Officer. John Wheatley

Gulab Singh & Sons, Calcutta—No. 22 Army C.—5-8-14—1,07,000.

Army Form Ó. 2118.

WAR DIARY
or
INTELLIGENCE SUMMARY.

(Erase heading not required.)

Instructions regarding War Diaries and Intelligence Summaries are contained in F. S. Regs., Part II, and the Staff Manual respectively. Title pages will be prepared in manuscript.

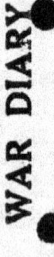

Hour, Date, Place.	Summary of Events and Information.	Remarks and references to Appendices.
10th Oct. '14. Oleans.	BOODON M. Boudon appointed our Interpreter - vice M. Vassas. V.A.S.C. Drivers vice Lupais by O.C. Divisional Horse Train. Sent in return of those inoculated against enteric fever. All Officers down to O. of Initials present. No scout anyone have been inoculated yet. Sanitary Squad = 20 men arrives and were accommodated to the night - will leave tomorrow under Command of Capt PARKINSON to the Camp Sanitary Officer.	
11th Oct. '14. Oleans.	Received horses for 2 mule Officers & Interpreter. - also an extra A.T. Cart + 2 mules for Supply of Rations - this makes S.A.T.Carts & all three furnished from Supply Train. Lahore Divn. must maintain it.	
12th Oct. '14. Oleans.	Completing clothing & Equipt of men and furbishing up Equipment etc.	
13th Oct. '14. Oleans.	Adapting Ambce Wagons to take Indian Stretchers which are about 1" wider than the Wagon stretchers - Raised the sides of the box under Drivers Seat at level of the upper stretcher. Removed the horn under rifle racks and put rifle clips on the front corner of wagon roof. The older pattern wagons are not requiring any alteration. The rifle threads on the weapon floor in the Sockets for the butts.	
14th Oct. '14. Oleans.	Conference under Presidency of A.D.M.S. Lahore Divn. who explained various matters re Order of March, Security as well as the lines on which the F.O. Ambulance should work	D.L. Wilcock

Army Form C. 2118.

WAR DIARY
or
INTELLIGENCE SUMMARY.

(Erase heading not required.)

Instructions regarding War Diaries and Intelligence Summaries are contained in F.S. Regs., Part II, and the Staff Manual respectively. Title pages will be prepared in manuscript.

Hour, Date, Place.	Summary of Events and Information.	Remarks and references to Appendices.
15th Oct. 1914. Oran.	Drew from Ordnance Store eight Revolvers & for Aviator's Uniform. Purchase Sanitary Supplies divers Relief Fund (Rs 1500 placed at our Disposal by Sis. Indus. Relief Fund). Prime and Beatrice Stores (A) also two acetylene lamps for night work, as it is difficult to see with the old lamps- and Carbide as Column can be had further making from med. Transfer to St. Cap.	4
16th Oct. 1914. Oran.	Kit inspection. Sob'ied about a cartload of mules rep. 40. 2nd Blanket now issued to natives who may have in a wrap, until Great Coats are available. In Indian Lines issued for one with Field, and issued tents with abrat. 6 I can Baton Regt. 1 per Battery or Company. Book laid by St. John Amb: for out of II.R. Fund. Got 7 dog-40% Coffee, these up in Town.	
17th Oct. 1914. Oran.	Warned to entrain tomorrow. Commenced to rain about 6pm. Continued through the night.	
18th Oct. 1914.	Everything soaking. Camp a morass. Apple of one cart broke and we had difficulty in getting another. However we got to PORT. SEC. in good time and Sladed 70 Trucks with own Horses Vehicles 8 Dodge 10 and these Trucks we share I feared have difficulty in fitting them off. Again. Staff officer Orders! All in by 2.50 pm. and the Train left at 4.5 pm.	[signature]

Army Form C. 2118.

(13)

WAR DIARY
or
INTELLIGENCE SUMMARY.

(Erase heading not required.)

Instructions regarding War Diaries and Intelligence Summaries are contained in F. S. Regs., Part II, and the Staff Manual respectively. Title pages will be prepared in manuscript.

Hour, Date, Place.	Summary of Events and Information.	Remarks and references to Appendices.
19th Oct 1914. in the Train.	Nothing to note. An harassing mostly by side lines — via Bou LOGNE & CALAIS. Took all night between trainplaces.	
20th Oct 1914. LUMBRES.	Detrained at ARQUES. and ordered to march to LUMBRES. about 12 kilos. Got them in dark and billetted in grounds of Paper Factory. Found Soap and approach difficult but the men found lamps did good service.	
21st Oct 1914. ARQUES.	Was distributing inst Stores (being now a sort of Corps Depot) and Stores for 5 ambulances) when at 12.30 pm sudden orders for us to fall in on Place on the march at 7th & 13 ex to H Q Force HAZEBROUCK. about 12 kils. The other side of ARQUES. Rendezvous 7 pm. Guide from here at 1pm!. They have handicapped us Bundled up and got here at dark, and billetted in a distillery.	
22nd Oct 1914. HAZEBROUCK.	Marched a San and Amiens here about 2 (pm) Opened up in a house in main street. but no sick or wounded occurred.	Orders for METEREN.
23rd Oct 1914. HAZEBROUCK.	Halted for day and Gave men and horses a much needed rest.	
24th Oct 1914. ESTAIRES. for LE DRUMEZ.	QMG here 11am. Found Square afog for arrival of C in C. a Squadron of European Cavalry. marched part of ESTAIRES to LE DRUMEZ. and as moved. got them at dark getting men and wagons settled in — alteration of orders on to our destination near La Couve.	Ordered to ESTAIRES just as we were starting for METEREN.  7pm Onwards

Army Form C. 2118

WAR DIARY
INTELLIGENCE SUMMARY.
(Erase heading not required.)

Instructions regarding War Diaries and Intelligence Summaries are contained in F. S. Regs., Part II, and the Staff Manual respectively. Title pages will be prepared in manuscript.

Hour, Date, Place.	Summary of Events and Information.	Remarks and references to Appendices.
24th Oct 1914. LA CASAN nr. LOCON	½ Bearer Division detached with "C" Tent Sub Div. Remain at LE DRUMEZ. Remainder marched to LA CASAN near LOCON. S of ESTAIRES. Refilled en route at LESTREM and camped in a farm with LECOUCHE DELMAIRE on S side of Canal. Major GIBSON & Capt LANE remained with detached portion of hospital. Opened for sick & wounded. 3 tent sub div.	
25 Oct 1914. Same place.	Sent out with Major FRANKLIN about 4am into 2 motor lorries to fetch in 250 wounded Sikhs from a chateau very definitely described as being "somewhere towards" LA BASSEE with great difficulty. Indian lights are dark and rainy nights found the horse wounded there. Back to No 113 F.A. at LA GORGUE to find gun where his wounded were coming from. Back to LAVENTIE when I noted an Cpl fighting motor for ambulances passing. Reinstated the White horse. To LAVENTIE. Back to LAVENTIE & then got new Division as follows: them up from the Ref Aid Posts of 15th SIKHS, 57th PANJABIS, & 34th SIKH PIONEERS but by this time (about 2am) all but 11 had been got away and there was ample room in surgeon for them. All the C.B. Corp. hurried up in the lorries. Got home again at 5am. etc. All the convoy was due to the place of rendezvous of wounded at Sikhs known to Regts in the trenches. The Casualties also even greater or affected than leaving little over 100 —
		[signature]

Gulab Singh & Sons, Calcutta.—No. 22 Army C—5.8.14—1,07,000.

Army Form C. 2118.

WAR DIARY
or
INTELLIGENCE SUMMARY.

(Erase heading not required.)

Instructions regarding War Diaries and Intelligence Summaries are contained in F. S. Regs., Part II, and the Staff Manual respectively. Title pages will be prepared in manuscript.

Hour, Date, Place.	Summary of Events and Information.	Remarks and references to Appendices.
25th Oct Contd. LA CASAN.	The collection of wounded from the front should not be done by Officers Commanding F.Ambulances. I went out as ordered A.D.M.S. – Asked F.O.ing to move on to LA GORGUE vice my F.A. together.	O. sent about 10 officers to other LA. in LA GORGUE.
26th Oct. 1914. LA CASAN.	Resting here, ready to move to-morrow to the last named place.	
27th Oct 1914. LA GORGUE	This place is about 2 kil[s] east of ESTAIRES. Here Capt Lane (LANE) had one last sub-division often as a hospital in the MAIRIE. We are billeted in a house opposite. We arrived at 10 a.m. Sent at night Sergt-Major FRANKLIN wounded & 7 with 20 Bearers to accompany No. 7. 13. F.A. 15 NEUVE CHAPELLE. No more wounded came in during the night. We evacuated Col. RICHARDSON & Capt. COMBE 47th SIKHS during the afternoon to BETHUNE. Total at 12.30 p.m. –	
28th Oct 1914. Same place.	Up at 6 a.m. Organized operation Room and extend[ed] G.1. PRINCE. Shell (Shrapnel bullet lodged) in abdomen. Received on 25th inst Shot rest of bullet near towards liver upwards and outwards from another line. He is doing satisfactorily. Surg Genl MACPHERSON visited hospital – and I lent his attention to a case of unattempted self-inflicted cases – Admitted Lieuts RAIT. KERR and NOSWORTHY 70 Co. R.E. wounded at NEUVE CHAPELLE. Former in I. Fore arm. Latter not in other. The latter it of R. Thumb. Shot Rt. amputated to first joint – 3 Sikhs admitted with wounds of left palm. Suspicion of self-infliction, palm blackened & ends shaken and located finger of two and deposits circumstances. Arranged with A.D.M.S. for the night and day parties of our Amb to 111 & 113 I Ambees should work in shifts so that personnel and horses may have regular rest	18 British Indian admitted. 10 Indian " "

[signature]

Army Form C. 2118.

WAR DIARY
or
INTELLIGENCE SUMMARY.

(Erase heading not required.)

Instructions regarding War Diaries and Intelligence Summaries are contained in F. S. Regs., Part II, and the Staff Manual respectively. Title pages will be prepared in manuscript.

Hour, Date, Place.	Summary of Events and Information.	Remarks and references to Appendices.
29th Oct 1914. LA GORGUE.	Justin 6 British and 41 Indian Troops accommodated the latter in personnel in rear of the square. No glass in windows. Have obtained fortunately oil and blankets. Provided much difficulty in getting. The natives too extravagant. Atta not now available. Gave milk to all.	
30th Oct 1914.	Admitted Lt LAURIE Seaforths. Lieut. DOBBIE 9th Bhopal Batt. Lt PAULSON Manchesters and MAJOR GIBBS 34th Pioneers. Also 56 prisoners Native Ofcs. Meninjis wound of upper extremities and 18 British sick and wounded. Pte DOWLING Wilts Regt compd fracture femur GSW. has become septic. He was wounded on 27th trying to hang on (?) B.F.A. But I fear there is little hope for him. He nearly dies on the operation. Would not stand operation. Drains and given stimulants re. The thigh is becoming gangrenous.	
31st Oct? 1914.	Evacuation of sick and wounded has been going on steadily since 28th inst and we have got rid of 44 British to BETHUNE (officers) and 110 Indians (officers) to BAILLEUL. Three Officers were also sent back to base BETHUNE. We have now only 1 Br. Officer, who will be fit in a day or two and two orderly men—	

Jno W Weeverto

Army Form C. 2118.

WAR DIARY
or
INTELLIGENCE SUMMARY.

(Erase heading not required.)

Instructions regarding War Diaries and Intelligence Summaries are contained in F. S. Regs., Part II, and the Staff Manual respectively. Title pages will be prepared in manuscript.

Hour, Date, Place.	Summary of Events and Information.	Remarks and references to Appendices.

War Diary of the Officer Commanding
No 6 British Field Ambulance
Lahore Division
I. E. Force —
for the month of
November 1914.

No 3 Section
A. G's Office at Base
I. E. Force
Passed to Secn S, Secn
on 10.12.14

PP 17622
Volume I

Army Form C. 2118.

WAR DIARY
or
INTELLIGENCE SUMMARY.

(Erase heading not required.)

Instructions regarding War Diaries and Intelligence Summaries are contained in F. S. Regs., Part II, and the Staff Manual respectively. Title pages will be prepared in manuscript.

(1)

Hour, Date, Place.	Summary of Events and Information.	Remarks and references to Appendices.
Nov 1st 1914. LAGORGUE AT ESTAIRES.	Arrear Racing rid of gangrene of R. thigh. Supervening on a G.S. wound. Used the room in which he had been twelve disinfected in Hotel Sanitary Conditions. Shaw buried and all precautions taken to prevent infection of future occupants.	
Nov 2nd 1914 Same place.	Lt. Col. STRICKLAND slight scalp wound 2nd Lt. MASSIE G.S.W., L. forearm L. foot & St. PAULSON Contusion Abdomen & Knee. All of the 2nd R. and one Other. fine. admitted. The two former joined to Clearing Hospital. Latter may be fit in a few days - 3 Other Ranks A.S. Corps. attached to Native Cart Cooks Wagon - 2 Taken on 2 R. F.A. Corps for Qui.s. men attached to employment the Sheep Pen.	
Nov 3rd 1914 Same place -	Drove continue same, Amb 5 & recover 3 with 1/2 Bearer Dist. work at night to 2nd E in Prangerie (WANGERIE) evacuating wounded from the Reg. Aid post of Manchester R. from here they pass to LE DRUMEZ and a dressing station and an hospital by motor Ambulances to the Text Division. They are then attached to and forward to receive a motor to the Clearing Hospitals, generally rent morning. The road to the Reg. Aid post is often under shell fire and only sufficient numbers of A.S. Corps. are taken out to handle the wounded, as there is not sufficient cover behind the trenches -	Sheet 4. ST. OMER. Kt. 4. 'X' Dance Sheet
Nov 4th 1914 Same place	Arrangements for collecting wounded and sick same as for last night.	
Nov 5th 1914 - idem -	Same routine. We now receive wounded on alternate nights with No T.S.A. while alone of personal resting - Major C.B. DYERS R.T. Corps. admitted Contusion abdomen & pelvis hematuria (told his horse while rolling him) Rev. K.G. FOSTER. C.o.F attached to no temporarily -	

[signature]

Army Form C. 2118

WAR DIARY
INTELLIGENCE SUMMARY.
(Erase heading not required.)

Instructions regarding War Diaries and Intelligence Summaries are contained in F. S. Regs., Part II, and the Staff Manual respectively. Title pages will be prepared in manuscript.

Hour, Date, Place.	Summary of Events and Information.	Remarks and references to Appendices.
Nov. 6th 1914. LA GORGUE.	Orders Broken Syringes to local analgesia (from DOWN BROS, with office of Eucaine, Novocaine and Adrenalin — Same routine as last night.	
Nov 7th 1914. Same place.	Received order to return of Bearer Section D from LE DRUMEZ. Hospital visits by Lieut. Gen. MACPHERSON & Major GOODBODY, IMS. Rec'd Supply of Stationery and 20 Service Post Cards — Our work at Front will be taken over by No 14 Field Amb: (ENGLISH)	
Nov. 8th 1914. Same place.	Bearer Section D under Major R. J. FRANKLIN, returned to H.Q. 25 of 7 Amb:	
Nov 9th 1914. Same place.	Continue to receive sick and wounded from front but in smaller numbers. Preparing Packages so as to be ready in case of a sudden order to move.	
Nov 10 Tu 1914. Sailleul	Sent in return of sick by Corps which have found thro' this FO. Amb: since our hostilities commenced — i.e. evacuated to their hospitals or does not include recoveries returned to their Corps. Total 139.—	
Nov 11th 1914.	Capt Sur'g'n Bouché sent to Comm Rangen vice Cap't Surg. Pell sick — Cap't Reg't GILLESPIE returned from detachment on relief by a MO.	
Nov 12th 1914.	All wounds of all hands, especially the left hand, are to be referred to the opinion of the D.M.S. as to whether there is any likelihood of their having been self inflicted. This is in order of G.O.C. and none of a suspicious character an to be evacuated without orders.	

[signature]

Army Form C. 2118

19

WAR DIARY
or
INTELLIGENCE SUMMARY.

(Erase heading not required.)

Hour, Date, Place.	Summary of Events and Information.	Remarks and references to Appendices.
Nov. 13th 1914 LA GORGUE	Nothing unusual to report —	
Nov 14th 14.	Rec'd orders from D.D.M.S. to send out "Beauvais" Dur: with 3 ambulance wagons to Les Drumez father this night to assist in evacuating the Regt. Aid posts of that area of our front. She wounded to go to No 7. B.T. Sent Capt ZANKIWILL and Surg. BLAKER+GILLESPIE. Late at night when orders came, wet and nasty —	
Nov 15th 14	Orders for concentration of unit: tonight for a move tomorrow. Rations and made ready. — Nothing saw two cases of S.S.W. left hand i.e. Ptes Turner and Cunningham Coy R. The former stated he was wounded by a comrade's rifle in a retirement from one trench to another. He lodged two muzzles of the rifle and where it exited three doubts as to life. The latter stated his rifle was resting against side of trench he was replacing a round bag when he was struck. Both were bandaged around the wound but I do not think the appearance could warrant a definite opinion that they were self inflicted.	
Nov 16th 9/14.	Orders to move to LOCON. <del>were</del> Congestion of traffic on road delayed our departure until 2pm. reached our destination at 3.30pm Got settled in and at 7.35pm. We received orders to be ready to move tonight. Packed up and stood by. Orders cancelled about midnight. We are to open here for sick only. Very poor accommodation. Could not possibly deal with very/sure wounded in this billet.	2/x Bld. Sgt. A. Surt. 7 ARRAS. I I J. M. Wharton

Gulab Singh & Sons, Calcutta.—No. 22 Army C.—5-8-14—1,07,000.

Army Form C. 21
20

WAR DIARY
or
INTELLIGENCE SUMMARY.

(Erase heading not required.)

Instructions regarding War Diaries and Intelligence Summaries are contained in F. S. Regs., Part II, and the Staff Manual respectively. Title pages will be prepared in manuscript.

Hour, Date, Place.	Summary of Events and Information.	Remarks and references to Appendices.
Nov 17th 1914. LOCON.	Officers Sick. Very few admitted, mostly complaining. Keeping them in Reg'l. Billmouk etc. As these men have had a hard time in the trenches, we keep them over there to rest and then they either return to duty or if unable to do so are sent to clearing hospital, first evacuation.	
Nov 18th 1914. Same Place.	Nothing of note.	
Nov 19th 1914. ditto.	Nothing special. Took continued handstriking. Change of Division with Meerut in the fighting line necessitate change of billets to two other area of LOCON. None suitable being available we await orders from D.H.Q. Orders & Evening received from Div. D. of M. S. to stand by with first meals to our move — and to collect all sick & horses shod with first meals to our move — and to collect Div. of march. R & C Com. R. from LACOUTURE & LELOBE. German aeroplane came down in our lines and was captured with two officers. — Snow fell pretty heavily in the evening —	
Nov 20th 1914. Same place.	Nothing new.	
Nov 21st 1914.	Nothing new.	
Nov 22nd 1914.	Ordered to CHATEAU GORRE — 5.5 Kilometre towards towards Cuinchy.	Ref. Sect "A" France Sheet ARRAS I-A

Gulab Singh & Sons, Calcutta—No. 22 Army C.—5.8.14—1.07.000.

WAR DIARY
or
INTELLIGENCE SUMMARY.

(Erase heading not required.)

Army Form C. 2118

(5)

2/

Instructions regarding War Diaries and Intelligence Summaries are contained in F.S. Regs., Part II, and the Staff Manual respectively. Title pages will be prepared in manuscript.

Hour, Date, Place.	Summary of Events and Information.	Remarks and references to Appendices.
23rd Nov. 1914. CHATEAU GORRE.	Marched at 12.30 p.m. Several parties came down from the first ride when going afterwards. Olan forces arr. Arrived 3 pm and found 130 9.F. & 2 Section No 20 B.F.A. Thin and very much in need to be attacked. We rendered all the assistance we could. Informed Offrs. when Div'n the situation and as the 9 Anvers mentioned above before present Div'n and am being withdrawn tomorrow we were steps to re-lieve them and bring up peaching further down – Although the night we were fully occupied – mainly Indian troops opposite the Cavalry.	
24th Nov. 1914. ditto.	Took away all cases not evacuated, and sent four wounded Indians by Indian troops – 130 9.F.A. + 2 Section No 20 moved out to ZELOBES. Have found billets in LES CHOQUAUX near LOCON in case we are withdrawn.	
Nov. 25th 1914. LES CHOQUAUX	Rec'd Orders this morning to evacuate and close, and then move to new billets. Did so – closed all up 6.9 am and tents in return all arrived after that time were attended and detained to be taken over by No 111 9.F.A. which is on its way here to carry on – Left here at 11. Rinfrom behind to hand them over and marched at 1.40 pm. We reached LES CHOQUAUX, 2 Kil. from LOCON at 2.30 and billeted about the village. Billets bad and hard to find – much scattered. Here we remain closed and resting – BETHUNE was shelled as we passed by and two shells fell about 200 yds from our column.	

Army Form C. 2118

WAR DIARY
or
INTELLIGENCE SUMMARY.
(Erase heading not required.)

Hour, Date, Place.	Summary of Events and Information.	Remarks and references to Appendices.
Nov 26th to Nov 30th LES CHOQUAUX	Resting at this place. During this time have taken the opportunity to draw money and pay such of the establishment, British and Indian who needed it. Over hauling equipment, greasing wagon wheels and completing deficiencies as has occupied our time - Goat Skin Coats have been supplied for British Native personnel also woollen gloves. Leather driving gloves will be supplied Calcutta drivers of Ambee wagons and Baggage Cart - A Report by Lt.Col. Moohea Commanding No 130 I.F.A. regarding my action in not at once relieving him on my arrival at CHATEAU GORRE, will in an unfavorable comment on my acting was received by the G.O.C. MEERUT DIV. was passed on to me for my report. This I sent in; but the correspondence is too long to incorporate in this diary. It will no doubt appear in the Diary of the A.D.M.S. LAHORE DIV. with his remarks on the subject -	

John Wherty
Lt.Col. R.A.M.C.
O.C. No 8 B.F. Amb.

Army Form C. 2118

WAR DIARY
or
INTELLIGENCE SUMMARY.
(Erase heading not required.)

Instructions regarding War Diaries and Intelligence Summaries are contained in F. S. Regs., Part II, and the Staff Manual respectively. Title pages will be prepared in manuscript.

Hour, Date, Place.	Summary of Events and Information.	Remarks and references to Appendices.
Dec 14	War Diary of Lt.Col. T.Dn.B. Whaite. O.C. No 8 British Field Ambulance for Dec. 1914. = 1 to 31. With 19 Appendices. Copies of Operation orders received from Brigade. Volume I Pp 23 6-28	

Army Form C. 2118

23

WAR DIARY
or
INTELLIGENCE SUMMARY.
(Erase heading not required.)

Instructions regarding War Diaries and Intelligence Summaries are contained in F. S. Regs., Part II, and the Staff Manual respectively. Title pages will be prepared in manuscript.

Hour, Date, Place.	Summary of Events and Information.	Remarks and references to Appendices.
Dec 1st 1914. LES CHOQUAUX.	Resting. Rec'd orders to search HINGETTE for suitable billets. Rest in. Found them at farm of M. BRETON on bank of canal close to Swivel bridge on East side.	Appendix 1
Dec 3rd 1914. HINGETTE.	Moved to above billets and continued our rest. Horse No 74 was destroyed W.V. Off' on account of internal injuries, got entangled in his head rope and cast loose. Had to dig pits for back stop RPs and the Per. Personnel. Neither mess out mined.	Appx. 2
Dec 4th to 16th HINGETTE.	Continued to rest. Rec'd orders latter date to 11th Dec to move to Chateau GORRE on 13th inst.	
Dec 13th CH&ATEAU GORRE.	Moved to Chateau GORRE and offered to reception of wounded. Sent out Major FRANCKLIN & Lt BIGGAM with 4 wagons & sufficient A.B.s to Le PLANTIN, whence they collected wounded. Roads are narrow and broken up. Vehicles cannot pass easily, one must get more or less bogged — hence we must went with supply and Amm'n Carts have returned from the front. No 113 I.F.A. 2 Sections are also and then are working at FESTUBERT. We all assist in dressing wounded when convoys return. —	Apx 3 & 4. 2 British wounded evacuated.
Dec. 14th 1914. Same place.	Arrangements same as last night as regards position & resource bearers but as there is a keen attack expected special arrangements for dealing with casualties were made verbally with no O C. Stretches. Operations cancelled late to-wire. Major Hogge By'r Pioneers a/c visited with Bomb wounds. Save 1500 units Anti Tet. Serum.	

O.C. 57B F.A.

Army Form C. 2118

24

WAR DIARY
or
INTELLIGENCE SUMMARY.
(Erase heading not required.)

2

Instructions regarding War Diaries and Intelligence Summaries are contained in F. S. Regs., Part II, and the Staff Manual respectively. Title pages will be prepared in manuscript.

Hour, Date, Place.	Summary of Events and Information.	Remarks and references to Appendices.
Dec 15th/14. BEUVRY.	Orders sent out from A.D.M.S. at 10 a.m. reached me at 5 p.m. A.B.C. messenger to Glanie. Had to hurried up but 2 sections more up. At 2 to BEUVRY leaving Major FRANKLIN and Lt BIG. AM behind under command of Major BRADLEY No 113 I.F.A. - We arrived about 7 P.m. and took over Boys School which was vacated today by No 12 I.F.A. - 'A' + 'B' Sections with me - Sent out Capt LANE at night to collect wounded from S. Side of Canal at a point ½ mile west of A in AUCHY-LEZ-LA BASSÉE which the rendezvous has been arranged. Some native regiments will also send their cases across from N Side of canal as too swampy to clear from CHOGORRE area is too swampy to clear from LE PLANTIN area.	Appex. 5. " Appex 6.
Dec 16th 1914. BEUVRY.	Rendezvous same as last night; Big attack effected but did not develop. Casualties practically nil. Wagons cleared Auxin Posts before 6 a.m. in morn:	Appex. 7.
Dec 17th/14 BEUVRY.	Rendezvous same - Wagon Bearers remained there all night returning at 6 a.m. 142nd Regt of French in reserve to the Centre Rouges at Auchy Reg Cabaree. - Same rumour about -	Appex. 8.
Dec 18th/14. BEUVRY.	Same rumour - shells from 11" I.F.A. remained here all night and ambulance motor also. Rendy. up by 6.50 a.m on 19th nothing unusual occurred.	HWWilliams Lieut Col Ramc O.C. 8FST A.

Army Form C. 2118.

WAR DIARY
or
INTELLIGENCE SUMMARY.

(Erase heading not required.)

Instructions regarding War Diaries and Intelligence Summaries are contained in F. S. Regs., Part II, and the Staff Manual respectively. Title pages will be prepared in manuscript.

Hour, Date, Place.	Summary of Events and Information.	Remarks and references to Appendices.
Dec 19th 1914. BEUVRY.	Had news of many casualties amongst Indian Corps. Sent out 3 wagons and bearers travois in bringing them in. Only 2 British casualties came in this morning.	5 British wounded 7 Br. Sick – 0 Indian – Appendix (1)
Dec 20th 1914. BEUVRY.	Wounded commenced to come in in considerable numbers after midday. Cleared out another room at the building and another in front. My two sections rejoined me from CHATS GORRE as the place was heavily shelled – Dreary wounded sent through the night and evacuating to C.C.R's. The majority of the casualties were Manchester Regt. We had also 28 wounded from native Regts. 7 whilst out were evacuated during the return. French wounded were also brought in to my hospital and attended to until they could be sent to their own hospital in BETHUNE.	Capt Bauer ROBERTS, 4th Sqn R.S. R.Khan – severely. R Shmeder + Thigh – 11 other Indian wounded Lt LYNCH, Manch.R. G.S.W. Sl. 2/Lt HORNELL (from R. Newcastle) 52 wounded to 44 evacuated 2 Died in R. Appendix (10)
Dec. 21st 1914. BEUVRY.	20 native sick came in at 10am were sent off to 112 I.F.A. The regiment at the front am being relieved by the 1st Division. Major Harold went out with Lt PEDLER R.A.M.C. to show him the ground and positions and had lunch. He is No 1 F. Amb. 1st Divn – all through the night casualties came in. 14 Corps were represented in our beds and altogether 98 wounded were treated and 83 evacuated. 5 officer cases through on rounds. All cases treated with 1/50 milk tebanhi antitoxin, except a few which were badly in a condition to bear it –	Major HITCHENS/Manch.R. 1st A. Capt. ROSE, both G.S.W. O Thigh (high) Capt CAVENDISH G/Shrops. G.S.W. dual + back Rangoons. Lt/Cpt McEWEN 1st Cam. H.Brs. G.S.W. Pelvis Revn – Relnr R Wdg 2/Lt STANTON, J. G.S.W. abdom. Seven Lt BARSTON. 13 Sikhs. Dislo. Shuldr 2/Lt Hon. R. NORTON 1/Scotts Gds Sprain back. Appendix (11)

Army Form C. 2118.

WAR DIARY
or
INTELLIGENCE SUMMARY.

(Erase heading not required.)

Instructions regarding War Diaries and Intelligence Summaries are contained in F. S. Regs., Part II, and the Staff Manual respectively. Title pages will be prepared in manuscript.

Hour, Date, Place.	Summary of Events and Information.	Remarks and references to Appendices.
Dec. 21st 1914. BEUVRY. cont.	All time casualties occurred in the fighting for the possession of the village of GIVENCHY — and it was very severely contested on both sides.	
Dec. 22nd 1914. BEUVRY.	21 cases received and 22 came in during the Day. 10 were evacuated — one died of wounds and one dying (unfit to move). Sitting remained when we received orders to clear and move to ALLOUAGNE 2½ miles west of CHOQUES and open there for reception of British sick 4 wounded of the LAHORE. Divn. Report of arrival to ADMS at LOZINGHEM. Sent Capt LANE & interpreter in advance to secure billets.	Map. ARRAS. 80,000 — Appendices (12) & (17) Appendix 18
Dec. 23rd 1914. ALLOUAGNE.	Moved off at 12 Noon. and marched via BETHUNE avoiding main roads through that Plan. Left 2 wounded at No 1 F. Amb. en route and passed via FOUQUIERES & CHOQUES. to Pont du REVEILLON when we left main road. On reaching ALLOUAGNE we found that no arrangements had been made for our accommodation & the JULLUNDUR Bge has taken up all the available billets. This being a rainy district there are no camps where the Native personnel can be accommodated — With great difficulty I managed to get the personnel housed for the night and tomorrow morning will try and get the CERCLE CATHOLIQUE which is now partially occupied by the 47 Sikhs. Raining & damp.	
24 Dec. 1914. ALLOUAGNE.	Moved into CERCLE CATHOLIQUE and spent forenoon — 10 came in Motor Amb's collects sick from the outlying villages and brings them here. We then evacuate and not likely to get to Train in 2 or 3 days — The LAHORE Division is now resting in this area —	Lieut. Col R.A.M.C. O.C. S.B. Field Amb.

Army Form C. 2118.

WAR DIARY
or
INTELLIGENCE SUMMARY. (5)

(Erase heading not required.)

Instructions regarding War Diaries and Intelligence Summaries are contained in F. S. Regs., Part II, and the Staff Manual respectively. Title pages will be prepared in manuscript.

Hour, Date, Place.	Summary of Events and Information.	Remarks and references to Appendices.
Dec 25th 1914. Xmas Day. ALLOUAGNE.	We had 16 patients in hospital on Xmas Day and I purchased a leg of pork and sausages with fresh bread & we gave them as good a Xmas dinner as possible. Plum pudding arrived from the Illing Fund – also from the King & Queen Xmas cards which were distributed to all. No evacuations to-day.	Weather frosty and fields quite white.
Dec. 26th 1914. ALLOUAGNE.	Princess Mary's Xmas presents arrived and distributed to all in Clearing Stn patients in half. 16 men admitted up to 9am this morning. 10 evacuated – 1 sent to duty – leaving 21 in half.	10 evac to Cl. R.
Dec. 27th 1914. Same Place.	Received 200 blankets. 200 warm pyjama suits – 200 warm bedsocks. 200 bedroom slippers – asked for a mule cart to carry these along when we move, but no extra transport will be allowed – sent in report on contents of same and reply to AQMG's memo re distinguished Gallant Conduct.	13 cases evacuated to Clearing Hosp. no one remained.
Dec. 28th 1914. Same Place.	Divided the above hospital clothing amongst the sections equally. Hope we shall be able to carry it along.	5 Cases evacuated to Lieut. Col. Hope of CLLRS.
Dec 29th 1914. Same Place.	Nothing special to report. A.D.M.S. Lahore Divn. proceeded on 7 days leave to England. Officials for him.	3 to duty 32 remain in hosp. Governments Heat. Rain.

Army Form C. 2118.

28

WAR DIARY
or
INTELLIGENCE SUMMARY
(Erase heading not required.)

Hour, Date, Place.	Summary of Events and Information.	Remarks and references to Appendices.
Dec 30th 1914. ALLOUAGNE	Instns. to 2nd Lt. Major GIBSON & FRANKLIN granted 7 days leave to England from this date inclusive —	16 cases evacuated 24 remain in hosp.
Dec 31st 1914. ALLOUAGNE	Drew F. rats for interval — " " 1750 for 2 days of personnel — New Years eve. Damp and cold —	

John Wiart
O.C. No 813 F.

"A" Form.
Army Form C. 2121.

MESSAGES AND SIGNALS

Prefix	Code		Charge	This message is on a/c of:	Recd. at	m.
Office of Origin and Service Instructions.		Sent			Date	
		At	m.	Service.	From	
		To				
		By		(Signature of "Franking Officer.")	By	

TO { O.C. 8 B.F.A. ① }

Sender's Number	Day of Month	In reply to Number	AAA
116	1st Dec" 14		

Please go to HINGETTE in the morning tomorrow and search for a suitable billet for a field Ambulance to rest in.

True copy
Tom Williams
Lieut-Colonel
O.C. No. 8 British Field Ambulance.

From
Place **LOCON**
Time

Sd/ B.B. Grayfoot
Col Ims
ADMS. Sahrinder

"A" Form.
Army Form C. 2121.
MESSAGES AND SIGNALS

| TO | No 8 B.F.A. | ② |

| Sender's Number | Day of Month | In reply to Number | |
| 123 | 3rd Dec '14 | | AAA |

Your unit should march tomorrow at 9 am to HINGETTE to take up billets at that place AAA Please place upon arrival to this office in LOCON AAA

True copy
John Williams Lt. Colonel
O.C. No. 8 British Field Ambulance.

Sd J.M. Sloan
Maj
for ADMS

From
Place LOCON
Time 10.35 am

"A" Form. — MESSAGES AND SIGNALS. — Army Form C. 2121.

TO: O.C. 8th F.A. HINGETTE (3)

Sender's Number: 161. Day of Month: (Dec) 11th AAA

Your unit will move to CHATEAU GORRE on 13th AAA Meerut Division FIELD AMBULANCE will vacate CHATEAU GORRE in time for you to take over by 12 midday and open for reception of sick and wounded AAA Orders for evacuation of sick and wounded will be sent later.

True copy
[signature] Lieut Col
O.C. No. 8 British Field Ambulance.

From: A.D.M.S. Lahore Division
Place:
Time:
Sd/ R B Gray Foot Col
ADMS

"A" Form.   Army Form C. 2121.
MESSAGES AND SIGNALS   No. of Message_____

| Prefix. Code m. | ds Charge | This message is on a/c of: | Recd. at _____ m. |
| Office of Origin and Service Instructions. | Sent At ___ m. To ___ By ___ | Service. (Signature of "Franking Officer.") | Date_____ From_____ By_____ |

TO { Lt Col. T. DuB. WHITE RAMC
     OC Mixed Field Ambulance ④
     CHATEAU GORRE

| Sender's Number | Day of Month | In reply to Number | AAA |
| 175 | 13 (Dec) | | |

You will be in Command of the mixed Field Ambulance at CHATEAU GORRE A.A.A. Your Bearer Division should clear the trenches north of the canal A.A.A. Rendezvous for waggons and bearers should be in the neighborhood of Cross Roads at E in RUE de of RUE DE BETHUNE at 6 pm A.A.A. You should get in touch with units of SIRHIND & JULLUNDUR Bdes a list of which and their position has been given you A.A.A. Reference map MERVILLE – LA BASSEE. Scale 1/40,000

True copy   *O.C. No 8 British F:c:d Ambulance*
                J. Dunwhaite

From   Adms, Lahore Division
Place   S/ B.B. Grayfoot
Time   Col
                     Adms
The above may be forwarded as now corrected. (Z)

Censor. | Signature of Addressor or person authorised to telegraph in his name

"A" Form. Army Form C. 2121.

MESSAGES AND SIGNALS   No. of Message _____

Prefix ____ Code ____ m.	Charge	This message is on a/c of :	Recd. at ____ m.
Office of Origin and Service Instructions.	Sent		Date ____
	At ____ m.	Service.	From ____
	To		
	By	(Signature of "Franking Officer.")	By

TO — O.C. No 8 B.F.A.   ③

| Sender's Number | Day of Month | In reply to Number | AAA |
| 182 | 15 (Dec) | | |

You should proceed at once with your unit less sections under Major FRANKLIN & LIEUT BIGGAM to BEUVRY to site at present occupied by No 112 J.F.A. and open there for reception of sick and wounded. AAA The two sections left at CHATEAU GORRE will be temporarily under command of O.C. No 113 J.F.A. AAA Report arrival to this office —

Noll.
Sent out at 10 A.M. Received at Bruno 5 P.M.

True copy
Toussaints   O.C. No. 8 British F.C. Ambulance.   *Boudier*

From A.D.M.S. Lahore Division   J H Sloan
Place ....   Major
Time ....   /a ADMS

The above may be forwarded as now corrected.   (Z)

Censor.   Signature of Addressor or person authorised to telegraph in his name
*This line should be erased if not required.
3562 M. & Co. Ltd. Wt. W929/549—100,000. 6/14. Forms C2121/10.

"A" Form. Army Form C. 2121.

MESSAGES AND SIGNALS

Prefix.	Code	ds	Charge	This message is on a/c of:	Recd. at	m.
Office of Origin and Service Instructions.		Sent			Date	
		At	m.	Service.	From	
		To			By	
		By		(Signature of "Franking Officer.")		

TO	O.C.	No 8 B.F.A.		(6)
		BEUVRY		

* Sender's Number	Day of Month	In reply to Number	AAA
185.	15 (Dec)		

Your Ambulance Wagons and bearers of the two sections at BEUVRY should rendezvous tonight half a mile west of AUCHEZ-LEZ LABASSEE on the BEUVRY LABASSEE Road at 6pm You will receive assistance from No 7 B.F.A. & No 112 I.F.A. concerning which verbal instructions will be given you tonight A.A.H. Scale map one over forty thousand

True Copy
Townshend Lieut Colonel
O.C. No. 8 British Field Ambulance.

From	A.D.M.S. Lahore Division
Place	
Time	S.D. Bigfoot Col A.D.M.S.

The above may be forwarded as now corrected.   (Z)

Censor.   Signature of Addressor or person authorised to telegraph in his name

*This line should be erased if not required.

"A" Form.   Army Form C. 2121.
MESSAGES AND SIGNALS   No. of Message ____

Prefix Code m.		Charge	This message is on a/c of:	Recd. at ____ m.
Office of Origin and Service Instructions.	Sent			Date ____
	At ____ m.		Service.	From ____
	To ____			By ____
	By ____		(Signature of "Franking Officer.")	

TO — O.C. 8/8 F.A.   BEUVRY   (7)

Sender's Number	Day of Month	In reply to Number	AAA
200	(Dec) 17		

Rendezvous for bearers and wagons as for last night AAA
You should get touch with Regt. aid posts of troops
of FEROZEPORE Bde south of
Canal i.e. Connaught Rangers AAA
Your wagons and bearers should
remain at Rendezvous till 6 am
AAA 142nd Regt of French Regt
in reserve to Connaught Rangers
at OUCHY-LEZ-LABASSÉE.

True copy
[signature]
O.C. No. 8 British F.d. Ambulance.

From Adms
Place
Time 4 pm

S. Biffen Foot
Col
Adms.

The above may be forwarded as now corrected.   (2)

Censor.   Signature of Addresser or person authorised to telegraph in his name
*This line should be erased if not required.

"A" Form.   Army Form C. 2121.

MESSAGES AND SIGNALS

TO: O.C. No 8 B.F.A. BEUVRY   (8)

Sender's Number: 207
Day of Month: 18 (Dec)

Rendezvous for wagons and bearers as for last night. AAA Bearers and wagons from 112 I.F.A are being detailed to rendezvous at BEUVRY where they will be available if required. AAA These should be accommodated in your unit for the night. AAA Refilling point tomorrow same as today.

"True copy"
Toussaint to
Lieut. Colonel
O.C. No 8 British Field Ambulance.

From: ADMS Lahore Division.
Place:
Time: 3.3 pm

"A" Form. Army Form C. 2121.

MESSAGES AND SIGNALS. No. of Message _____

Code ___ m.	W___	Charge	This message is on a/c of:	Rec'd ___ m.
and Service Instructions.	Sent			Date _____
	At ___ m.		Service	From _____
	To			By _____
	By	(Signature of "Franking Officer.")		

TO { O.C. No 8 B.F.A. BEUVRY. (9)

| Sender's Number | Day of Month | In reply to Number | AAA |
| 219 | 19 (Dec) | | |

Rendezvous for bearers & wagons
for last night A.A.A.
Refilling point unchanged

True copy
[signature]
O.C. No. 8 British Field Ambulance.

From A.Durs. Labon Division
Place
Time 4.30 pm

Lt B [signature]
Colonel
ADMS

The above may be forwarded as now corrected. (Z)

Censor. Signature of Addresser or person authorised to telegraph in his name

*This line should be erased if not required.

3662 M. & Co. Ltd. Wt. W929/549—100,000. 6/14. Forms C2121/10.

"A" Form. Army Form C. 2121.

MESSAGES AND SIGNALS. No. of Message _____

Prefix _____ Code _____ m. | W | Charge | | Recd. at _____ m.
Office of Origin and Service Instructions. | Sent | | This message is on a/c of: | Date _____
_____ | At _____ m. | | Service. | From _____
_____ | To _____ | | _____ | _____
_____ | By _____ | | (Signature of "Franking Officer.") | By _____

TO { OC. No 8 B.F.A. (10)

| Sender's Number | Day of Month | In reply to Number | AAA |
| 223 | 20 (Dec) | | |

Rendezvous for Bearers and Wagons
same as last night. AAA
Large numbers of wounded may
be expected.

True copy
Tom Dillon
Lt. Colonel
O.C. No. 8 British Field Ambulance.

From Adv. Lahore Divn.   S. M. Sloan
Place   Major
Time 4.15 pm
The above may be forwarded as now corrected.   (Z) for ADMS.
                                    Censor.   Signature of Addressor or person authorised to telegraph in his name
*This line should be erased if not required.
3662 M. & Co. Ltd. Wt. W929/549—100,000. 6/14. Forms C2121/10.

"A" Form. Army Form C. 2121.

MESSAGES AND SIGNALS   No. of Message_____

Prefix____ Code____ m. / ds / Charge This message is on a/c of: Recd. at____ m.
Office of Origin and Service Instructions. Sent Date____
____ At____ m. Service. From____
____ To____ ____ ____
____ By____ (Signature of "Franking Officer.") By____

TO { O.C. No 8 B.F.A.   ⑪

* Sender's Number | Day of Month | In reply to Number | AAA
  231 | 21 (Dec) | |

Send bearers and wagons to rendezvous to BEUVRY-LA BASSEE Road half a mile to west of junction AUCHY-LEZ LA BASSEE Road map one over forty thousand - A.A.A. British wounded to No 8 B.F.A. & Indian to No 112 I.F.A. A.A.A. one Government Motor Ambulance will be at the Rendezvous -

True copy
Tom Richards Lieut-Colonel
O.C. No. 8 British Field Ambulance.

From Adms Lahore Div. Sgd M Sloan Major
Place
Time 1.15 pm
        for Colonel Adms
The above may be forwarded as now corrected. (Z)

Censor. Signature of Addressee or person authorised to telegraph in his name
*This line should be erased if not required.
3662 M. & Co. Ltd. Wt. W929/549—100,000. 6/14. Forms C2121/10.

"A" Form. Army Form C. 2121.

MESSAGES AND SIGNALS.

No. of Message _____

Prefix	Code	m.	Words	Charge	This message is on a/c of :	Recd. _____ m.
Office of Origin and Service Instructions.			Sent At ____ m. To ____ By ____		____ Service. (Signature of "Franking Officer.")	Date ____ From ____ By ____

TO — O.C., No 8 B.F.A. ⑫

Sender's Number	Day of Month	In reply to Number	AAA
1175	22 (Dec)		

Many wounded are lying in Regl aid post Connaught Rangers Send four horse ambulance wagons at once to evacuate wounded to your unit.

True copy
Townshend
Lieut. Colonel
O.C. No. 8 British Field Ambulance.

From ADMS Lahore Div'n
Place
Time 355 (pm)

B B Gray ??
Colonel
ADMS

The above may be forwarded as now corrected. (2)

Censor. Signature of Addressor or person authorised to telegraph in his name

*This line should be erased if not required.

"A" Form. Army Form C. 2121.
MESSAGES AND SIGNALS.

TO: O.C. No 8 B.F.A. Ⓑ

Sender's Number	Day of Month	In reply to Number	AAA
238	22 (Dec)		

Rendezvous for bearers and wagons same as last night.

True copy
Tom Edwards
Lieut-Colonel
O.C. No. 8 British Field Ambulance.

From: Adms Lahore Div
Place:
Time: 4.10 pm

Sd/ T.W. Grayfoot
Colonel
Adms

"A" Form. Army Form C. 2121.

MESSAGES AND SIGNALS

No. of Message _____

Prefix ____ Code ____ m. Ns Charge This message is on a/c of: Rec'd. at ____ m.
Office of Origin and Service Instructions.
Sent Date ____
At ____ m. ____ Service. From ____
To ____
By ____ (Signature of "Franking Officer.") By ____

TO O.C. No 8 B F.A. (114)

Sender's Number: 241 | Day of Month: 22nd (Dec) | In reply to Number | AAA

Your bearer division is to remain at the rendezvous until recalled from this office A.A.A. Send an officer with your bearer division at once to AUCHY LES LA-BASSEE A.A.A. Large number of wounded in aid posts of Coldstreams and Scots Guards. A.A.A. Aid Post of Manchester Regt. on S side of Canal should also be evacuated tonight. A.A.A. British wounded to your unit, Indian to No 112 I.F.A.

True copy
[signature] Lieut-Colonel
O.C. No. 8 British Field Ambulance

From A.Dens Lahore Div. [signature] B.M. Grayford
Place Col
Time 5:30 pm ADMS

The above may be forwarded as now corrected. (Z)

Censor. Signature of Addressor or person authorised to telegraph in his name

*This line should be erased if not required.
3662 M. & Co. Ltd. Wt. W929/549—100,000. 6/14. Forms C2121/10.

"A" Form.   Army Form C. 2121.
MESSAGES AND SIGNALS   No. of Message _____

Prefix __ Code __ m.	___ds Charge	This message is on a/c of:	Recd. at ____ m.
Office of Origin and Service Instructions.	Sent		Date ____
	At ____ m.	____ Service	From ____
	To ____		
	By ____	(Signature of "Franking Officer.")	By ____

TO { O.C., No 8 B.F.A.   (15)

| Sender's Number | Day of Month | In reply to Number | AAA |
| 212 | 22 (Dec) | | |

No 1 Field Ambulance now open in School by Railway line ½ mile W of BETHUNE Railway Station on North Side and close to the line. AAA Despatch all wounded now coming in from your front to this field ambulance.

True copy
Tom Williams
Lieut-Colonel
O.C. No 8 British Field Ambulance.

From Adms. Lahou Divn   B S Shappool
Place   Col
Time 7.20 pm   Adms
The above may be forwarded as now corrected.   (Z)
                                 Censor.   Signature of Addressor or person authorised to telegraph in his name

*This line should be erased if not required.

"A" Form.   Army Form C. 2121.
MESSAGES AND SIGNALS.   No. of Message_____

Prefix____ Code____ m.   W   Charge
Office of Origin and Service Instructions.   This message is on a/c of :   Rec'd at____ m.
                                                                                      Date____
                          Sent
                          At____ m.   ____Service.   From____
                          To
                          By   (Signature of "Franking Officer.")   By

TO – O.C. No 8 B.F.A.   (16)

Sender's Number | Day of Month | In reply to Number | AAA
243 | 22 (Dec) | |

2 Motor cars herewith sent to help in the evacuation of the add posts South of canal – AAA Send responsible person to conduct them to AUCHY, and to inform the med. officer of your Bearer Division of their arrival AAA. British wounded to be disposed of as in my operation order 242 and Indian wounded to No 112 I.F.A. vide my operation order 241 of date

True copy
John Wheat Lieut-Colonel
O.C. No. 8 British Field Ambulance

From Adms Lahore Divn
Place
Time 10.25 pm   Wrayfoot
                                      Colonel
The above may be forwarded as now corrected. (Z)   Adms

                          Censor. Signature of Addressor or person authorised to telegraph in his name
*This line should be erased if not required.

"A" Form.   **Army Form C. 2121.**

MESSAGES AND SIGNALS

No. of Message _____

Prefix	Code	ds	Charge	This message is on a/c of:	Rec'd at ___ m.
Office of Origin and Service Instructions.		Sent At ___ m. To ___ By ___		Service (Signature of "Franking Officer.")	Date ___ From ___ By ___

TO — O.C. No 8 B.F.A.   (17)

Sender's Number	Day of Month	In reply to Number	AAA
246	22		

Refilling point tomorrow same as today time 8am. AAA Division is moving tomorrow prepare to move tomorrow to ALLOUAGNE about 2½ miles W of CHOQUES. Time of movement will be communicated to you later AAA map one over eighty thousand.

True copy
Yours truly,
Lieut.-Colonel
O.C. No. 8 British Field Ambulance.

From Adv's Labour Div'n
Place
Time 11 pm

18/3 Playfair
Colonel
ADMS

The above may be forwarded as now corrected. (2)

Censor.   Signature of Addresser or person authorised to telegraph in his name

This line should be erased if not required.

3662 M. & Co. Ltd. Wt. W929/549—100,000. 6/14. Forms C2121/10.

"A" Form. Army Form C. 2121.

MESSAGES AND SIGNALS

TO O.C. No 8 B.F.A.

(18)

Sender's Number: 253
Day of Month: 23

AAA

Your unit should be closed and march to ALLOUAGNE 2½ miles west of CHOQUES today where you will open for reception of sick. An officer being sent in advance to select necessary accommodation A.A.A. Report of your arrival should be sent to me at LOZENGHEM.

True copy
Yours (?)

Lieut-Colonel
O.C. No. 8 British Field Ambulance.

From: Adms Cavalry Div?
Time: 8.25

Adms

WAR DIARY
OF
No 8 British Field Ambulance.

From 1st January 1915 To 31st January 1915.

121/4401
Jan 1915

Army Form C. 2118

WAR DIARY
or
INTELLIGENCE SUMMARY.

(Erase heading not required.)

Hour, Date, Place.	Summary of Events and Information.	Remarks and references to Appendices.
Jan. 1st 1915. ALLOUAGNE.	Capt. LANE R.A.M.C. who is temporarily in m/c charge of 1st Batt. in and Refr. in the absence of Capt. BURNEY R.A.M.C. on leave, is ordered to be ready to accompany Batt. if they move at short notice. — Paid out to 1859 to personnel. — Recommended No 3039 Naick ACHROO Army Bearer Corps to offered recognition for his conduct on the night of 28th Oct '14. at PICANTIN while B Section Bearer Division were removing wounded from Vital Place to FAUQUISSART. Shot fired, he rallied the trenches men under heavy fire from machine guns and rifles. — He advanced in stretching the Bearers under trying conditions. — At BIGGAM R.A.M.C. were in command of the Bearers on this occasion. — Also brought to the notice of the A.D.M.S. Lahore Division the following Officers and Warrant Officers for consistent good work since this unit took the field. Major R.J. FRANKLIN R.A.M.C. who between 31st Oct + 7th Nov. Collected the wounded from ROUGE CROIX under shell and rifle fire, night after night, assisted by Asst. Surg's. H.A. FOX S.M.D. Asst Surg's E.O. JOHNSON, + G.R. FIDO S.M.D. Capt. LANG reported that the late Asst. Surgeon showed great coolness and resource while collecting wounded in the LE PLANTIN area on 14th Dec '14. on which occasion a wounded man being brought in on a stretcher was again wounded by rifle fire. — Receiving sick from Lahore Division. J.W.B. Watts Lt. Col. R.A.M.C.	Evacuated - 7 Remaining 7. Note :- * No 3039 Naick ACHROO awarded D.C.M.

Army Form C. 2118.

WAR DIARY
or
INTELLIGENCE SUMMARY.

(Erase heading not required.)

Instructions regarding War Diaries and Intelligence Summaries are contained in F.S. Regs., Part II, and the Staff Manual respectively. Title pages will be prepared in manuscript.

Hour, Date, Place.	Summary of Events and Information.	Remarks and references to Appendices.
Jan 2nd 1915. ALLOUAGNE.	Continued open for sick - Nothing Special to note -	Evac? 8, Remains 10.
Jan 3rd/15. Same place	nil. Chiefly abrasions of feet & rheumatic pains -	Evac? 7, Rem? 24.
Jan 4th/15. do do	nil -	evac? 11 " 25.
Jan 5th/15. " "	nil -	" 11 " 25.
Jan 6th/15. " "	Major Franklin returned from leave. Lt. Biggam went on leave	" 10 " 24
Jan 7th/15. " "	My Ayrshire Wagons to collect sick from Regts. of Jullundur Bde British Cochem as usual. Natives to H.Q. 9.7.D. -	" 16 " 24
Jan 8th/15. " "	nil.	" 12 " 21
Jan 9th/15. " "	Drew 192 francs pay of personnel and 12/6. Bal? Imprest up to 6.1.10. Major Gibson who was home on leave returned to head Quarters. 14 O.R.s leave expired. Board on account of absentees absence -	" 9 " 17
Jan 10th/1915. " "	nil.	" 9 " 15
Jan 11th/15. " "	Inspection of Baggage Wagons by Corps Commander -	" 3 " 22
Jan 12th Tues/15. " "	nil.	" 4 " 28
Jan 13th Wed/15. " "	nil.	" 8 " 24
Jan 14th Th/15. " "	Drew fr. 750. for pay of British Personnel.	" 3 " 39

J.W. Wheats,
Lt Col RAMC.

Army Form C. 2118.

WAR DIARY
or
INTELLIGENCE SUMMARY.

(3)

(Erase heading not required.)

Instructions regarding War Diaries and Intelligence Summaries are contained in F. S. Regs., Part II, and the Staff Manual respectively. Title pages will be prepared in manuscript.

Hour, Date, Place.	Summary of Events and Information.	Remarks and references to Appendices.
Jan 15th/15 ALLOUAGNE.	Paid British Personnel. Withdrew coats warm & blouses from A.S.C. & W.B.C. These with some khaki drill garments will be handed to D.O.P. in commission to Indian base (order Dec G.Y.G.) John Gair Pvt Date French R.G.S.W. Palm left hand, while cleaning his rifle in billets. Suspicious case. Seen by O.C. G.Y.G.	Evac? 1 Officer & 12 men Sens? 1 Officer & 12 men Rein? 47.
Jan 16th/15 Same place -	Nothing Special to report -	Evac? 17. Rein? 41
Jan 17th/15 Same place -	Major Gibson returned to Unit. Officers on leave by Med. Board vide Jan 9/15. We are now keeping men longer in hospital and thereby save some wastage from firing line.	Evac. 3 Rein? 51
Jan 18th Same place.	nil -	evac 14 Rein? 41.
Jan 19th/15 do -	7. M.B.C. 1 Pakhali Dhotie. +1 No orderly joined for duty - (re-enforcements)	" 3 " 37.
Jan 20th/15 do.	nil -	" 3 " 42.
Jan 21st/15 do	nil	" 5 " 43.
Jan 22nd/15 do.	nil -	" 6 " 44
Jan 23rd/15 do -	Lt. A. Wilson temp. R.A.M.C. joined for duty. Stood first coat night.	" 4 " 44
Jan 24th/15 do -	2/Lt. P. McDonald 64 Bat. R.F.A. Recent promotion transferred with heavy influenza - 2 Indian Spares received - Lt. A. Wilson R.A.M.C. ordered to 4th Brit Seaforth Highldrs.	Evac. 1 Officer 3 men 26.
Jan 25th/15 do.	Orders received to be near to move at 2 hrs notice (Order No 34) Later orders to be in constant readiness - (order 35) Cancelled later and we revert to 2 hr readiness 2hr notice - Lt. Two returns to No. 8137A. on enquiry.	Evac. 2 Rein? 35. Apps I, II & III signed JWRaven or. 8137A.

Gulab Singh & Sons, Calcutta—No. 22 Army C.—5-8-14—1,07,000.

WAR DIARY
INTELLIGENCE SUMMARY
(Erase heading not required.)

Army Form C. 2118.

Instructions regarding War Diaries and Intelligence Summaries are contained in F. S. Regs., Part II, and the Staff Manual respectively. Title pages will be prepared in manuscript.

Hour, Date, Place.	Summary of Events and Information.	Remarks and references to Appendices.
Jan 26th/15 Aupugne	Still prepared for move - All leave for officers cancelled -	Off IV & V Evac. 8. Rem. 32.
Jan 27th 1915. Dampier	Case of Measles admitted. Pte Wilson 32nd Brigade Co. Doctors about 20 contacts and put 20 animals in hospital - There have been 4 cases among children in their billet since 1 Jan. Infant still in scarlet a house with children in the village of Rozingham with a clean wife of heather. Clearing billets & took precautions.	Evac 12. " 30 Ap. VI
Jan 28th 1915. Cont? Dampier	We are now attached permanently to the JULLUNDUR 13th Bde AREA with 112 J.F.A. the combined Fd Amb Co under my command. Sadar SMO. 15DE. Half officers unit is to Jullundur R.D. Mr Marshall with Ferozpore Bde working in conjunction with 111 J.F.A. under Col. Frost JMS, Oc. of officers - Major Gibson Capt Lane will be with detached 2 Sections.	Ap. VI Evac 3 Remain 42
28 Jan 15. Dampier	We still continue in a state of preparedness varying in intensity as the Jullundur Bde is on brief.	Evac 3 (1 Rem 42 Officers)
Jan 29th/15 Dampier	Under orders from A.DMS. we returned to Ordnance Department 8. hole tents. their lifetime over. Major by 12:30/06 - Drew FS 739 1st Corps 1st Bde British Peril.	Evac. 17 includes 2nd cat Off.2 Off M. VII Remain 32
Jan 30th/15 do -	As Ferozpore Bde is now compared wholly of Indian troops we in reserve. My unit will not be divided. For this am thankful. We are to move on mon. 1st (rec - Case of Measles from MARLES. R.A. of Staff. Came in 20 today - this was a man contacted. 13 officers + 2 officers pneumonia - Took usual precautions.	Evac? 1 officer 7 men Rem. 2. 39.
Jan 31st/15 do.	Made all preparations for evacuation of sick for the move. But of measles case to No 4 Cav. Cl. Station - and arranged for disposal of sick while away from the Regiment - many men have sore feet and cannot march. These will not march. Those will be transported to new Billets either by motor lorry or in the amb. wagons. Asst Surgeons Johnson & Maj McCuen Asst Surgn Sick with Defective vision oliver fever. Left today to be fitted with spectacles at Shamakhara, much reduced Asst Surg Fido fever chest pain also evac to 54 Cav. Cl. Stat.	Evac? 1 9SMC audients " 61 sick Rem? 0 -

J.M.W. McNeil Lieut Col
O.C. 113 F.A. -

"A" Form.   Army Form C. 2121.

MESSAGES AND SIGNALS.

No. of Message ____

Prefix ___ Code ___ m.	Words	Charge	This message is on a/c of:	Recd. at ___ m.
Office of in and Service Instructions.	Sent			Date ___
	At ___ m.		Service.	From ___
	To ___			
	By ___		(Signature of "Franking Officer.")	By ___

TO { O.C. No 8 B.F.A.

| Sender's Number 54 | Day of Month 23 | In reply to Number | AAA |

Your Unit should be ready to move at 2 hours short notice AAA These orders are issued on account of the heavy gun fire heard this morning near BETHUNE AAA Be

From A.D.M.S. Lahore Divn
Place
Time

Colonel
A.D.M.S.

The above may be forwarded as now corrected.   (Z)

Censor.   Signature of Addressee or person authorised to telegraph in his name

*This line should be erased if not required.

Copy / 34

Operation order No 35
by
Colonel B.B. Grayfoot, A.D.M.S Lahore Divn.

LOZINGHEM
25-1-15

Reference map BETHUNE 1/40,000

1. A mixed field ambulance consisting of No 111 I.F.A. and 2 Sections No 8 B.F.A. under Command of Lt Col G.A. Frost I.M.S will be in Constant readiness to move.

2. Lt Col Frost will on receipt of orders to move report himself to the G.O.C Ferozepore Bde for orders and will act as S.M.O. of the detached force.

3. No. 112 I.F.A. will hold itself in Constant readiness to move from RAIMBERT to LOZINGHEM to take over the sick at present in No 111 IFA and to open for the reception of Indian sick of the Divn less detached force.

4. The OC. no 111 I.F.A. will detail one

Sub Asst Surgeon to remain with the sick of his Unit and to rejoin when these have been taken over by No 112 I.F.A.

Colonel IMS
ADMS Lahore Dist

c

Copy No 1 - to O.C. No 8 B.F.A.
2 - " " " 111 I.F.A
3 " " " 112 — "
4 " G.O.C. Ferozepore Bde
5 retained

Sent by Orderly & Motor Cyclist at 4.50 pm.

"A" Form.　　Army Form C. 2121.

MESSAGES AND SIGNALS.

TO	O.C. 8 B.F.A.
	O.C. 111 I.F.A.

Sender's Number	Day of Month	In reply to Number	AAA
499	25th	—	

Wire received from General Staff at 10 pm begins "G 376 Orders requiring Division to remain prepared to move at two hours notice and to certain units to be in a state of constant readiness are cancelled aaa Ferozepore Brigade (less 9th Bhopal Infantry) 5th Brigade R.F.A. 20th Coy S. & M's and 2 sections 8 B.F.A. and 111th Indian Field Ambulance will however remain prepared to turn out at two hours notice aaa Acknowledge ends.

From: A.D.M.S. Lahore Divn
Time: 10-10 pm

"A" Form. Army Form C. 2121.

MESSAGES AND SIGNALS.

URGENT

TO — O.C. No 8 BFA

IV

Sender's Number: 39
Day of Month: 26

AAA

Please hold your Unit in constant readiness to move aaa All leave cancelled.

From: ADMS Lahore Divn
Place:
Time: 7.10 pm.

Colonel
ADMS

"A" Form.
MESSAGES AND SIGNALS.
Army Form C. 2121.

TO — O.C. No 8 B.F.A.

Sender's Number: KO
Day of Month: 26th
AAA

Reference my 39 please detail two sections under your command to remain at ALLOUAGNE with all six ambulance waggons to go round the Divisional area and collect all sick British and Indian and to admit them to your two sections for evacuation AAA. There will be also left fifty-five small pox contacts of 15th Sikhs in 57th Rifles area LAPUGNOY and 80 mumps contacts of 9th Bhopals in LABOURIERE for which you should make medical arrangements as to inspection & treatment AAA. Sick not evacuated from No 111 FA to be taken over by you.

From: ADMS
Time: 4-35 pm

"A" Form.

MESSAGES AND SIGNALS.

TO: OC NO 8 BFA

Sender's Number: 44
Day of Month: 27
AAA

my	39	of	yesterday	aaa
the	state	of	constant	readiness
is	relaxed	to	one	of
being	able	to	turn	out
at	two	hours	notice	

From: ADMS Lahore Divn

Time: 9.20 am

for Colonel

Copy/ 66
VII

Operation order No 48
by
Colonel B.B. Grayfoot, A.D.M.S. Lahore Div.
d/- 29-1-15

Reference map BETHUNE 1/40000

1. The Jullundur Brigade having been ordered to relieve the Ferozepore Brigade as Brigade on duty from 5 p.m. today and to remain ready to move at 2 hours notice, a mixed field Ambulance consisting of No 112 I.F.A., and 2 sections No 8 British Field Ambulance under the command of Lt Col. J. du B Whaite R.A.M.C, will be in readiness to move at 2 hours notice

2. On the Brigade being ordered to move the Officer Comdg the mixed Field Ambulance will report himself to the G.O.C. ~~Lahore~~ Jullundur Bde.

3. Two I.M.S. Officers have been detailed from No 111 I.F.A. to join No. 112 I.F.A., to complete the establishment

establishment.

[signature]

Colonel M.S
A.D.M.S Lahore Divn

Copy No 1 to O.C. No 8 I.F.A
       2 to O.C. No 112 I.F.A
       3 to G.O.C Jullundur Bde
       4 Retained

Sent by Orderly & Motor Cyclist at 5.55 pm

Serial No 35

121/4719

WAR DIARY
with appendices.

No 8 British Field Ambulance.

From 1st February 1915 To 28th February 1915

121/4719
Feb.15.

MESSAGES AND SIGNALS.

TO: SMO Bde (8th BFA)
112th IFA

Sender's Number: 911-B
Day of Month: 7th
AAA

Lahore Divn wires begins No 8 British Field Ambulance less 1 Section and 112 IFAmbulance should march for LOCON on tenth passing CALONNE at 8.30am ENDS For necessary action route to be taken LE PETIT PACAUT - PARADIS - LA TOMBE WILLOT AAA Addressed SMO Jullundur Bde repeated 112 / IFA for information

No 3 Section
C's Office at Base
I. E. Force
Passed to _____ S. Sect'n
on _____

From: Jullundur Bde
Place:
Time:

"A" Form. Army Form C. 2121.

MESSAGES AND SIGNALS.   No. of Message _____

Prefix ____ Code ____ m.	Words / Charge		Recd. at ____ m.
Office of Origin and Service Instructions.	Sent	This message is on a/c of:	Date ____
	At ____ m.	Service.	From ____
	To ____		By ____
	By ____	(Signature of "Franking Officer.")	

TO { OC. NO 8 B F A
     „ NO 112 I.F.A.   app II

| Sender's Number | Day of Month | In reply to Number | AAA |
| 04 | 20 | | |

The field Amb under your Command will march from LOCON on 23 February 15 to CALONNE by LACROIX MARMUSE — L'EPINETTE Square Q-12-C AAA Starting point LOCON 8.30 am for NO 8 B F A aaa NO 112 I F A will follow immediately in rear

From ADMS Lahore Divn
Place
Time

The above may be forwarded as now corrected.   (Z)
                                   Censor.   Signature of Addressor or person authorised to telegraph in his name
                                                                      Colonel
                                                                      ADMS

*This line should be erased if not required.

158 S.B. Ltd. Wt. W5673/619—50,000. 10/14. Forms C2121/10.

"A" Form.   Army Form C. 2121.
MESSAGES AND SIGNALS.

Prefix	Code	m.	Words	Charge		This message is on a/c of:	Recd. at	m.
Office of Origin and Service Instructions.			Sent				Date	
			At	m.		Service.	From	
			To					
			By			(Signature of "Franking Officer.")	By	

TO { O.C. No 8 B.F.A.   App VIII

| Sender's Number | Day of Month | In reply to Number | |
| 67 | 22 | | AAA |

On the 23rd February your Unit will continue its march beyond CALONNE to St FLORIS

From ADMS Lahore Divn
Place
Time

The above may be forwarded as now corrected. (Z)

Censor.   Signature of Addressor or person authorised to telegraph in his name

Colonel
ADMS

66

From O.C. 8 I.B.F.A.
To A.D.M.S. Lahore Dw⁻

Will you kindly issue orders as
to when you wish another Section
to proceed to Ham?
I wish to insert the order in my War
diary.
Yours obediently
22/2/15.   Scott Ramsay.

O.C. no 8 B.F.A.
      another
The ^Section No 8 B.F.A. should
proceed to Ham on the 24th Feby 15.

                    MMGrey Col
                    Colonel AMS
                    A.D.M.S. Lahore Divn
69
22-2-15

Army Form C. 2118.

WAR DIARY
or
INTELLIGENCE SUMMARY.
(Erase heading not required.)

Instructions regarding War Diaries and Intelligence Summaries are contained in F. S. Regs., Part II, and the Staff Manual respectively. Title pages will be prepared in manuscript.

Hour, Date, Place.	Summary of Events and Information.	Remarks and references to Appendices.
ALLOUAGNE to ST. FLORIS. Feb. 1st 19.15.	Marched at 8.20 a.m. and fell in, in our place in Column of Platoons B Coy at the West end of the village. As usual there was considerable confusion caused by 2nd Line transport of other units blocking the way at every cross roads. Visited at 10 m.15 to each from few minutes and were always met closed up. Arrived at ST. FLORIS at 1 p.m. and prepared to open in Mairie and the school adjoining. Found however that the school was still in use and as there was not sufficient accommodation in the Mairie I represented the matter to the B. Que Commanding July. O. He visited the place and arranged that the other village school which had been taken to the March. R. a billet should be evacuated & all the children taught there and the school next the Mairie handed over to me. At our last place we had straw mattresses made with hurdles and these we carried along in the ambulance wagons and there was no delay requisitioning straw for patients. The road from ST. FLORIS Church to the AIRE - LABASSÉE canal was over billeting area and with some trouble we got all accommodated. I can accommodate 40 cases. We carried along 20 men & March. Res. unable to march through foot trouble and handed them over to their unit on arrival. The B. Ce is in Reserve still and liable to turn out at 2 hrs. notice in support of Meerut Div. so we have only spent one section of 2 Section with No. 112. J. F. A. will go if needed. A/Sd. Lieut. FIDO rejoins us en route. A/S. Lieut. JOHNSON still away.	Admitted 1 Evac. d 0 Remain 2

John W. ...therson

WAR DIARY
INTELLIGENCE SUMMARY
(Erase heading not required.)

Army Form C. 2118.

Instructions regarding War Diaries and Intelligence Summaries are contained in F. S. Regs., Part II, and the Staff Manual respectively. Title pages will be prepared in manuscript.

2

Hour, Date, Place.	Summary of Events and Information.	Remarks and references to Appendices.
ST. FLORIS. Feb. 2nd/9/15.	A case of Cerebro-Spinal meningitis having occurred in 3rd RIFLES at Allouagne, the contacts here are isolated in tents – 3 officers have been but no definite symptoms. I have secured a horse for the closed cases of men in British units. All other have been taken to make interior of Coy Staff and the horses of contacts here. R.Q.M.S. Lahore will deal fully with the matter no doubt. I have done all I could as S.M.O. July & Be.	Admitted, evac. Rem? 5 – 0 – 7
Same place. Feb 3rd/9/15.	All Cerebro-Spinal contacts evacuated (by A.D.M.S. order) to No. 4 Con. C.H. Station LILLERS for a Bacteriological examination. No cases here so far. Received 16 Lentillerre tent, Lowry for use with cavalry. – All the old (Belgian oil lanterns were too damaged for further use were abandoned at Blaringhem –	1 Offr. – 2 2 men – 6 1 Offr. – 2 5 men – 6 men
Same place. Feb. 4th/9/15.	Nothing Special.	2 – 1 offr. – 6 2 men
" " 5th "	nil	5 – 1 – 10
" " 6th "	nil	0 – 3 – 7
" " 7th "	At A.G. 13.15.a.m. Rome. ordered to Cairo for duty with 14 L.I.	1 – 3 – 5
" " 8th "	Capt. J.W. LANE. with one Section ('C') sent to H.A.M. for duty with Ferozepore Bde. (EN.ARTOIS.)	2 – 3 – 4
" " 9th "	nil. we march tomorrow –	1 offr. – 3 men – 4 men

John Wheatn Lt Col. Reeve

Army Form C. 2118.

WAR DIARY
or
INTELLIGENCE SUMMARY.

(Erase heading not required.)

Hour, Date, Place.	Summary of Events and Information.	Remarks and references to Appendices.
ST. FLORIS to LOCON — Feb 10th 1915	Major A.W. GIBSON R.A.M.C. ordered to LUCKNOW clearing station for duty as Sanitary Specialist — permanently. Lieut. Craine main Rgt. Franklin and myself alone in this Amb'ce. Marched at 9 a.m. behind Bde ambulance. much delayed by blocking of main front ahead owing to narrow soft roads — arrived LOCON at 1.30 p.m. Took over school on road running North from church when No 20 B.F.A. meerut Div'n F'd Amb'ce was open. A Dr'sg watched please. had been to Post Office when we were here before. Billets on road from school to Canal. S. of LOCON. Stores and your rations along this road. Mud seems bad as bad as ever. Secured a billet and a mess room for officers when we rejoined the store. We carried along 3 men from ST. FLORIS with no side —	Admitted. Sec. Remain. 1 Offr. 0 — 1 Offr. 3 men ——————————— App. I
LOCON. Feb 11th 1915	One of the three men has developed measles. the other two are now "Contacts." We evacuated the measles to MERVILLE. Vice Quartier this billet to O.C. No 20 B.F.A. at ST. FLORIS. also notified B. Square Maje third two Motor Cyclists left 7.30 a.m. (from which we are now latest) are also contacts. N.Z. Qr mount Division to here and will not leave until tomorrow. we take in sick from Sn Rns 19th and 18th hospn in Southern B.S. area. 3 wounded from Jt. J. and Conn R. brought in — The two H.L.I. of heart to come been hit by same bullet. Sharpnel making hinch. Conn R man hit in R. knee. 'ricochet' probable. recently adming and evacuated.—	7 — 1 Off't 7 — 1 Off't 4 men

Conulescents
F. Col. Ramm

Army Form C. 2118.

WAR DIARY or INTELLIGENCE SUMMARY.

(Erase heading not required.)

Hour, Date, Place.	Summary of Events and Information.	Remarks and references to Appendices.
Feb. 12th 1915. LOCON.	Furnished rooms occupied by G.O.C. Ivent into Dirt on account of influenza - men from Stores and Pre Coy. which made a most infectious fumes and Peroxide Noxide Roman A.D.M.S. arrived with Labor Dir. Staff.	Admitted Evac. Remains 10 br. 8 — 4 — 8 men
FEB 13th 1915. LOCON.	LT. A.G. BIGGAM. R.A.M.C. admitted from Med.Charge H.L.I. with Influenza. probably contacted from their Med. Aid Post. Previous Med.Officer had it.	3 br. 36 br. 11 men 2 br. 4 men 1
FEB. 14th 1915. Same place.	Nil.	1 br. 26 br. 5 men 10 men 4
FEB. 15th 1915. Same place.	Suspected case of Cerebro-Spinal meningitis brought in by Lt. ALCORN from the 3rd Co. Lahore Div. Train at FOSSE. A.D.M.S. came and saw him. No Strepto. but much cerebral irritation. Nervous increasing. Took in returning. He was transferred to STOVER, and the rooms disinfected, all steps re contacts taken — Men Men bars and faces personnel — vide 18.2.15.	10 br. 26 br. 11 men 7 men 16 br. 7 men
Feb. 16th 1915. Same place.	Nothing Special to note.	12 — 11 —
Feb. 17th 1915. Same place.	Asst. Surg. E.O. JOHNSON rejoined unit, having been filled with Details Glencorse	6 — 7 — 2 br. 6 men
Feb. 18th 1915. Same place.	Diagnosis of C.S. Meningitis confirmed in case noted on 15.2.15.	11 16 br. 16 br. 5 men 12 men
Feb. 19th 1915. Dainfler.	LT. A.G. Biggam taken off sick list, and returns to duty with this unit — LT. E.P. STRATFORD. R.A.M.C. arrived and posted to us —	6 — 9 — 1 br. 9 men

Norman Alford, Lt.Col. R.A.M.C

Army Form C. 2118.

WAR DIARY
or
INTELLIGENCE SUMMARY.
(Erase heading not required.)

Instructions regarding War Diaries and Intelligence Summaries are contained in F. S. Regs., Part II, and the Staff Manual respectively. Title pages will be prepared in manuscript.

Hour, Date, Place.	Summary of Events and Information.	Remarks and references to Appendices.
Feb 20th 1915. LOCON.	Nothing Special to report.	
Feb 21st 1915. Jour plein.	Recd. orders to move to CALONNE on 23rd inst. Changed a heavy wagon 1½ cwt. wgn. for a G.S. wagon. 1½ cwt. wgn – which weighs about 15 cwts to –	3 — 1 — 7
Feb 22nd 1915. LOCON.	School in CALONNE to which we were going will not be vacated by No. 1913 F.A. until Div. until 24th so we are therefore taken over old billets area in ST. FLORIS for one night.	0 — 4 — 3
Feb 23rd 1915. LOCON to ST. FLORIS.	Left LOCON at 8.30 am followed by No. 112 9th F.A. (who are proceeding to CALONNE) marched via LA CROIX MARMUSE & L'EPINETTE. We had to wait about 3hrs at a road junction for two batteries to pass by – arrived at S.T.F. at 1pm. Found infections disease affecting 90 contacts in C.S. Meerups belonging to 83rd Bath R.F.A. (who had case on 9th inst) and details of garrison other R.A. units. Leaves numbers in CALONNE. All billets marked once spirits. Recd. orders last night to remain here instead of moving to CALONNE.	1 — 1 — 3 A/M III A/M III
Feb 24th 1915. ST. FLORIS.	D Section sent to 11AM. under Major FRANKLIN to join 'C' Sect. already there. There is now half the Ambulance now detailed to FEROZEPORE Brian. A private follower. Syce (Nur number) H.Q.R.A. No. 3 Co. 1st Sappers and Miners died last night of some fatal malady, as the Circumstances were suspicious of C.S.M. a Pathan his service were applied for and contacts to separate. Civilian chiefs with meals in 3 tenants AU FAISAN GRIS. Put out of hounds contributed to NCO's group. John and the out – as the signature of the Bacillis has had their officers in common whine and presumably rend the estannet. LT. H.M. Mackenzie Rann reported attached to afternoon.	4 — 0 — 7 A/M IV

Army Form C. 2118.

WAR DIARY
INTELLIGENCE SUMMARY.
(Erase heading not required.)

Instructions regarding War Diaries and Intelligence Summaries are contained in F. S. Regs., Part II, and the Staff Manual respectively. Title pages will be prepared in manuscript.

Hour, Date, Place.	Summary of Events and Information.	Remarks and references to Appendices.
Feb. 25th 1915. ST. FLORIS.	Performed P.M. on Sye HIRA. Brain vessels intensely congested but no meningitis present. Sent specimen of cerebro spinal fluid to LILLERS for examination. Case of measles amongst the contacts RA. to C.S.M. reported malta.	Admitted - Sick - Remains 13 - 9 - 11
Feb 26th 1915. same place.	Nothing to report.	5 - 5 - 11
Feb 27 1915. same place.	Very cold, east wind. Nothing special tonight.	3 - 10 - 4
Feb. 28th 1915. ditto.	Wind continues cold. Rode over to HAM. and inspected C+D Sections. We have very comfortable and suitable billets and sufficient accommodation for sick. Capt. LANE goes back to LILLERS superintend the bathing arrangements for troops.	6 - 4 - 6
Note.	During this month we have had a comparatively quiet time, taking in local sick of Jullundur Bee. Whilst in ST. FLORIS, and the sick in Bethune Dist. Area Lahadin whilst at LOCON. Any wounded received have been casual occurrences.	

Yours Wheate
Trey Reeve
No. 8. F.A.

WAR DIARY

with Appendices.

No 8 British Field Ambulance: Lahore Division.

From 1st March 1915 to 31st March 1915

Army Form C. 2118.

WAR DIARY
or
INTELLIGENCE SUMMARY.
(Erase heading not required.)

WAR DIARY of Officer Commanding
No 8. British Field Ambulance.
LAHORE DIVISION,
for month of March, 1915.

(with 6.
Appendices)

Army Form C. 2118.

WAR DIARY
or
INTELLIGENCE SUMMARY.
(Erase heading not required.)

Instructions regarding War Diaries and Intelligence Summaries are contained in F.S. Regs., Part II, and the Staff Manual respectively. Title pages will be prepared in manuscript.

Hour, Date, Place.	Summary of Events and Information.	Remarks and references to Appendices.			
			Adm.	evac.	Res. Remg.
March 1st 1915. ST. FLORIS.	Rode over to BUSNES and found that 3rd Cavalry Sabre Divn has been abolished in future we shall obtain money from 2nd Cavalry at Indian Army Corps H.Q. Lt. JEFSON. R.A.M.C. evacd to Merville after slight N&mophiysis. Lt. MACKENZIE takes his place with H.L.Infy.	Sick Offr. 1 men 1	1 1	– 1	0 6
Mar. 2nd/15. – ditto. –	Cerebrospinal contacts of 83rd Batt R.F.A. have now finished their quarantine and may march off. 21 measles contacts remain here.	Sick Offr. – men 7	– 6	– 1	1 7
Mar. 3rd/15. – do –	Two men (ranchers) R.shattered by bombs which exploded during practise. Only slight wounds. Drew £r 3750 and paid personnel.	Sick Offr. 1 men 9	– 6	– 1	1 10
Mar 4th/15. – do –	I see by Gazette of Mar 1st /15. I have been promoted Colonel.	Sick Offr. 3 men 3	– 5	– 1	1 9
Mar 5th /15. – do –	Two children of the Mayor in whose house I am are our men and my billet have developed Mumps. They are segregated at the opposite end of the house and have not been in contact with any of our men. I left Father McGrath instructions as they pass through the Kitchen. Took precautions regarding and disinfection of all concerned with Eucalyptus Soleria Solution.	Sick Offr. 1 men 3	1 3	– 1	1 9
Mar 6th/15. – do –	Reported Mumps to A.D.M.S. Saline Divn. giving situation of house infected.	Sick men 4	3	–	10
Mar 7th/15. – do –	C &D Medico with Major FRANKLIN & Capt LANE rejoined the unit from HAM-en-ARTOIS. JULUNDUR Bde left and FEROZEPORE Bde marched in.	Sick men 18	3	–	25
Mar 8th/15. – do –	A case of measles has occurred in CONNAUGHT RANGERS. FEROZEPORE Bde. Mater Repolis and billets disinfected and marked. Also inhabitants. The Men occupied at LA MIQUELERIE. All contacts segregated.	Sick men 2	57	–	22

John Whurton.
Col. R.M.C.

Army Form C. 2118.

WAR DIARY
or
INTELLIGENCE SUMMARY.
(Erase heading not required.)

Instructions regarding War Diaries and Intelligence Summaries are contained in F. S. Regs., Part II, and the Staff Manual respectively. Title pages will be prepared in manuscript.

Hour, Date, Place.	Summary of Events and Information.	Remarks and references to Appendices.
March 9th 1915. ST. FLORIS.	Tomorrow move to LE CORNET MALO - and to remain there closed awaiting further orders. Drew Ft. 1000L. and paid some British and Indian Personnel. Settled about billets at new place and gave memo to Major re those occupied here. - Notably to have further bad weather! Returned the remainder of the Fur Coats to DADOS. Those with O's Section Handed over at LILLERS-bon-HAM.	Sick Admd. Evac'd. Died. Remg. Offrs. — — — — Men. 3 25 1 0 Appendix I
Mar 10th 1915. From ST. FLORIS TO LE CORNET MALO.	Marched at 7:30 A.M. via CALONNE & RUE DES VACHES. to LE CORNET MALO - arrived at 9.10 A.M. - map BETHUNE 1.40,000 Square Q.28 map BETHUNE 1.40,000 -	
Mar. 11th 1915. — do —	R.C. ordered 11 a.m. to send immediately bearer division with six Ambulance wagons and two officers to report to A.D.M.S. at Meerut Refat Centre at VIEILLE CHAPELLE, also Personnel of Cav't Division to assist No.19 B.F.A. at the Rendezvous. - By noon Major FRANKLIN, Capt. LANE, Lt. BIGGAM & Lt. STRATFORD, proceeded with: - 32 British Personnel. - 26 A+C+M, Indian R's 6 and 12 Majors, 3 A.T. Carts, and 30 stretchers - Remainder behind with Lieut. Johnson. The transport consequent. H. Baggage wagons, the Supply wagons & Extra Cart. The latter will take rations for this Detachment daily. — I shall draw its Camp and rations at our refilling point and send them out there — See Rec. P.Rg. FOSTER + the interprêt remain with him -	Appces II & III
	Note added subsequently re work of Bearer Division & Personnel of Cav't Division refuelled by Major R.J. FRANKLIN R.A.M.C. - Immediately on arrival the Personnel of the Tent Division turned to, to assist No.19 B.F.A. relieved their Personnel who went to the front that night, and enabled their captains + men to get some well-earned rest. The Bearer Division under Capt. J.W. LANE with Lt. ER. STRATFORD. Proceeded to the advanced Dressing Station - (at road junction known as DEAD TREE CORNER. S. 8 at. 1 in 40,000 BETHUNE MAP) arriving there at 5.45 P.M. and relieves the Bearer Div'n of No.19 B.F.A. Munroe had to carry 2 miles from the Regt'l Aid Posts along the Rue du Bois (a from the LABASSEE — ESTAIRES Road.) The Ambulance wagons worked from a 2½ miles from Co's Dressing Sation to Tent Division in VIEILLE CHAPELLE. The Rue du Bois, was under Still and artillery fire all the way but fortunately, no one was hit. Returns by No.19 B.F.A.	W.Abbott T.CoRawe

WAR DIARY
or
INTELLIGENCE SUMMARY
(Erase heading not required.)

Army Form C. 2118.

Hour, Date, Place.	Summary of Events and Information.	Remarks and references to Appendices
Mar.12th 1915. LORNE MALO.	Still waiting orders to move – Nothing special to report.	nil.
13th 1915 – Ma – 10/ VIEILLE CHAPELLE.	Rec'd orders to march with my M.D.O.S. to VIEILLE CHAPELLE via PACAUT – PARA DIS. arriving there by 9am. Messages sent off last night one reaching me this morning. At 7.15am. Much difficulty in getting bearers owing to left orchard. Arrived Wounded T|Cas'ts Evac. Sick. At 12 noon and took over from No 19 B.F.A. Meerut Div'n Major BARTLETT R.A.M.C. who left all unevacuated British wounded Sick as transfers also 1 German Off'r. + 21 Privates wounded – latter reported to G.S.O. I. of Division mentioning officers' requirements. He soon he sent down after interview. No 7. Mot. Amb. Convoy evacuated no twice daily or oftener if required – Convoy in command of Capt'n TURNER R.A.M.C. Rear Div'n continues to collect wounded from A.D.C. Dressing Station and airpost as noted in 11th march – Amb. went relieved at night by No 2. 13.F.A. Rear Div'n The latter one located as follows – on Rue du BOIS. LEICESTER Reg't. in dugouts at S.H.A. – Native reg't aid post in house about 5.10.a. – Rear Div't 8/112. I.F.A. woods to with native wounded. The following regts have been represented among't stores brought in during the fighting at NEUVE CHAPELLE. 1st Manch R. 2 Berks Bl'k Watch 4th Suffolk R. – 3rd London R. – and R.F.A. These were treated in A.D.V. Dressing Station.| Officers – 1 Men – 24 108 88 Appendix IV. German Off'r. – 1 Men – 21 5 25 Sick Off'rs – 2 Men – 31 22 1 17
Mar 14th – do –	Wounded continue to come in and are evacuated regularly by No. 7. M.A.C. Lt MAUNSELL R.A.M.C. left behind by Meerut Div'n notes to 110 Rat. R.F.A.	Wounded Off'rs – 2 Men – 30 58 2 16 Sick Off'rs – 2 Men – 27 36 2 9

Maunsell Col amc

WAR DIARY or INTELLIGENCE SUMMARY

Army Form C. 2118.

(Erase heading not required.)

Instructions regarding War Diaries and Intelligence Summaries are contained in F. S. Regs., Part II, and the Staff Manual respectively. Title pages will be prepared in manuscript.

Hour, Date, Place.	Summary of Events and Information.	Remarks and references to Appendices
Mar 15th/15. NEILLE CHAPELLE.	My Bearer Dis'n relieved No 9 B.F.A. at Nufront - Lt S. BIGG O.M. 4 STRATFORD for duty tonight - Wounded coming in, in reduced number -	Wounded Offr 1 Oth r 3 Exec 1 Recruits 1 Men 24 36 - 2 Sick Offr 1 1 - 0 Men 20 20 1 9
Mar 16th/15 -do-	Submitted tabular statement of wounded from time we took over Tent Dis'n on 13th inst. up to 14th Mar. showing German wounded separately. This information was asked for by Divn. Indian Army.	Wounded Offr 0 1 1 0 Men 25 14 7 12 Sick Offr 0 0 - 0 Men 15 10 1 15
May 17th/15 -do-	Lt. A.G. BIGG, A.M.R.A.M.C. slightly wounded by shell fire in left hand - No 112 F.A. Adv'd Dressing Station was shelled and some wounded killed and General R.B.C. also. Shrapnel after they had got out Also the wounded that remained killed a Capt. DUNBAR R.F.A. wounded Lt. Wigg. Detailed report sent in by A.D.M.S. 2nd D.W.D - The deeper wounds which come in, are now opened up when possible and swabbed out with pure carbolic acid & then washed with weak carbolic lotion 1 in 60 -	Wounded Offr 1 1 1 0 Men 31 28 - 14 Sick Offr 4 4 1 0 Men 13 16 1 11

Nowrolivla
Col ams

Army Form C. 2118.

WAR DIARY
or
INTELLIGENCE SUMMARY.
(Erase heading not required.)

Instructions regarding War Diaries and Intelligence Summaries are contained in F.S. Regs., Part II, and the Staff Manual respectively. Title pages will be prepared in manuscript.

Hour, Date, Place.	Summary of Events and Information.	Remarks and references to Appendices
Mar 18th 1915. VIEILLE CHAPELLE.	Work continues to progress smoothly. Mountain coming in now are few in number. Submitted approximate number of winter clothing articles which can be dispensed with during the Summer. Return Medical. Fur coats have gone. Return Great Coats. Probably identifiable, and afterwards warm under clothing which may be in afterwards kept into condition for storage against next winter. Additional number of stretchers with neighbouring Field units. Procured to treble the number of Stretchers also crowded out taken into the operation room for dressing etc.	Wounded. Admitted Evac.? Died Remaining Offr — 1 0 0 1 Men — 8 7 1 8 Sick → 2 0 — 2 Offr → — — — — Men — 17 14 — 14 Germans—2 1 — 1 wounded
Mar 19th 1915. —do—	Lt. STRATFORD. R.A.M.C. evacuated (ex poisoned wound, finger of left hand) with lymphangitis. Temp 99.4° — admitted for treatment. Lt. A.C. JEPSON. R.A.M.C. joined for duty in his place.	Wounded Adm? Evac. Died Remaining Offr — 1 1 — 0 Men — 6 7 — 7 Sick Offr — 0 2 — 0 Men — 17 8 — 27 19/3
Mar 20th 1915. —do—	One Officer with measles adm? from trenches (Lt. C.J.O. BERRINGTON, 13th Indian Lancers) and evacuated. Precaution steps taken —	Germans wounded Offr — 0 1 — 0 Men — 0 Wounded Offr — 0 1 — 0 Men — 7 4 — 10 Sick Offr → 2 2 — 0 Men — 21 7 — 26 20/3 J.W.W. Wheeler Col. A.M.S.

WAR DIARY
INTELLIGENCE SUMMARY.

Army Form C. 2118.

(Erase heading not required.)

Hour, Date, Place.	Summary of Events and Information.	Remarks and references to Appendices
Mar 21st/15 – VIELLE CHAPELLE.	Received order from D.M.S. (1st Army.) (No.673 of 18.3.15 para 2.) as evacuation of GSW cases of abdomen and other wounds which invariably are fatal, were much retained and loss of value rather Spite this two deaths in C.C.S. in this F.A. and so the greatest care is exercised to prevent the chance of such cases leaving when obviously unfit to be moved." Also inform no that there is an Advn Dressing Station of No. 2 Amb. Posn. to which badly wounded officers many and without the delay of passing through another F.A. and as 1st and Indian Corps & the one HT. Ca.O. & new Corps go to No. 6. C.C.S. LT. MACKENZIE, H.M. R.A.M.C. surely wounded left arm, while attending to casualties caused in H.L.I (Quickilsheivar M.O.) by shells dropped this billets – most of the wounded shown in remark column were men of this Battalion – LT. R.C. JEPSON. R.A.M.C. sent to take his place with H.L.I	**Wounded** ⟨Admit⟩ ⟨Evac⟩ ⟨Died⟩ ⟨Remain⟩ Officers 1 1 0 0 Men 26 24 5 7 **Sick** Officers 0 0 - 0 Men 12 23 - 15.
Mar 22nd/15 ditto.	Nothing Special occurred –	**Wounded** Officers 0 0 - 0 Men 3 2 1 8 **Sick** Officers 2 2 - 0 Men 6 6 - 10
Mar 23rd/15 – do –	Nothing Special Wrote –	**Wounded** Officers 0 0 - 0 Men 5 4 - 9 **Sick** Officers 7 0 1 1 Men 12 6 - 17

gonD Whistle Col. Amb.

Army Form C. 2118.

WAR DIARY

INTELLIGENCE SUMMARY.

(Erase heading not required.)

Instructions regarding War Diaries and Intelligence Summaries are contained in F. S. Regs., Part II, and the Staff Manual respectively. Title pages will be prepared in manuscript.

Hour, Date, Place.	Summary of Events and Information.	Remarks and references to Appendices
March 24th Vieille Chapelle	Col. Whait a.m. :- Granted on seven days leave to ENGLAND. Lieut. M.J. Warick reports himself for duty on transfer from No 7 B.G.T.A. Maj. G. Beauchaplain when chaplain by Capt Lane and Lieut Warwick transfer to 5th Rawalpindi Brigade. Mentioned in despatches collected Wounded and died from the Meerut Division had taken over trenches most of there occupied by the Lahore Division. The sick and wounded of the Julundur Brigade being attended by 130 G.F.A.	Wounded officers 0, other ranks 0, Sick/Died officers 0, other ranks 3, Remaining officers 0, other ranks 13 Sick- officers 1, other ranks 16, 0, 0 men 20, 0, 21 Appendix I
March 25th Calonne	Relieved by No 30 G.F.A. Meerut Division, and marched at 12.50 P.M. C + D Sections under Capt Barr Arrived to LE CORNET MALO Remain closed to further orders. A/B Sections marched to CALONNE & Report for duty. 101 cases of Sick & wounded their brought in two Ambulance Wagons	Wounded officers 0, other ranks 0, men 0, 8, 0, 5 Sick- officers 1, other ranks 0, 0, 0 men 3, 11, 0, 5 Appendix II
March 26th Calonne	A box containing military stores etc not required by the trains was sent to the forwarding office MERVILLE to be despatched to England.	Wounded officers 2, other ranks 3, 0, 4 Sick officers 1, other ranks 3, 0, 9
March 27th —	Lt. J.S. Waggons and 9 Horses were taken over from D.A.C. Three Wagons in place of 5 A.T.A. cart 5 Drivers & O.C. arrived with the carts.	Wounded men 0, 1, 0, 3 Sick officers 1, 1, 0, 0 men 4, 5, 0, 8

Army Form C. 2118.

WAR DIARY
or
INTELLIGENCE SUMMARY.

(Erase heading not required.)

Instructions regarding War Diaries and Intelligence Summaries are contained in F. S. Regs., Part II, and the Staff Manual respectively. Title pages will be prepared in manuscript.

Hour, Date, Place.	Summary of Events and Information.	Remarks and references to Appendices				
			Admitted	Evac.	Died	Remain
March 28th Column	Five A.T.A. carts with their Drivers were returned Bazgulla	Wounded men	0	0	0	3
		Sick men	3	7	0	4
March 29th. Do.	Four Khalsa Bhistis returned to India	Wounded men	0	1	0	2
		Sick men	4	6	0	2
March 30th. Do	Nothing to note.	Wounded sick	0	0	0	2
			4	4	0	2
March 31st. Do	Nothing to note	Wounded	0	0	0	3
		sick	2	1	0	3

Norris Wheaton
Col. Comd.

"A" Form.
MESSAGES AND SIGNALS.

Prefix	Code	m.	Words	Charge		This message is a/c of :	Recd. at	m.
Office of Origin and Service Instructions.			Sent				Date	
			At	m.		Service.	From	
			To				By	
			By			(Signature of "Franking Officer.")		

TO { O.C. No 8 B.F.A. *appvi*

| Sender's Number | Day of Month | In reply to Number | AAA |
| 80 | 9 | | |

evacuate your Unit to-day aaa your Unit will march tomorrow via CALONNE RUE DE VACHES to LA CORNET MALO Square Q.28 arriving there by 9 am. where you will remain closed awaiting further orders

From A.D.M.S. Lahore Divn
Place
Time 10 am

The above may be forwarded as now corrected. (Z)

Colonel
A.D.M.S

"B" Form.
MESSAGES AND SIGNALS.
Army Form C____

Prefix XB Code KA
Office of Origin and Service Instructions: YIC Priority
Words: 66
Received At 10.10 P.m. From YIC By Pte Reid
Office Stamp: YIC 11/3/15

TO: OC No 8 BFA Lieornet
malo sg 928

Sender's Number: 90
Day of Month: 11
AAA

Send immediately bearer division of your unit with six ambulance wagons and two officers to report to ADMS' at meerut report centre at VIELLE CHAPELLE also send personnel of tent divn to assist no 19 at VIELLE CHAPELLE aaa Addressed OC No 8 BFA repeated ADMS meerut report centre.

From: ADMS Lahore Divn
Place:
Time: 9.30 AM

"A" Form.

MESSAGES AND SIGNALS.

No. of Message ___

Prefix ___ Code ___ m.	Words	Charge	This message is on a/c of:	Recd. at ___ m.
Office of Origin and Service Instructions.	Sent			Date ___
___	At ___ m.		Service.	From ___
___	To ___			
___	By ___		(Signature of "Franking Officer.")	By ___

TO { O.C. Bearer Divn
     No 8 B.F.A.   Appnt. III

| Sender's Number | Day of Month | In reply to Number | |
| F 23 | 11 | | AAA |

Your ambulance waggons & bearer ~~division~~ will relieve those of 19 B.F.A. this afternoon at Advanced Dressing Station at Lead Tree Corner square S.8. line between a & b. aaa.

On being relieved by No 8 B.F.A. waggons and bearer division of 19 B.F.A. will return to VIEILLE CHAPELLE to rest aaa.

The waggons of No 8 B.F.A. will take the wounded to No 7 B.F.A. at R.13.b.

From A. Dir S Meerut Divn
Place
Time

The above may be forwarded as now corrected.   (Z) H Butler Major
                                                    for CRA
Censor.   Signature of Addressor or person authorised to telegraph in his name

*This line should be erased if not required.

3562 M. & Co. Ltd. Wt. W929/549—100,000. 6/14. Forms C2121/19.

(5132) Wt. W 2384-583. 8/14. 15,000 Pads. Wy. & S., Ltd.

A 24

"B" Form.   Army Form C 2122.

MESSAGES AND SIGNALS   No. of Message

Prefix SB	Code 7, ? P m.	Received	Sent	Office Stamp.
Office of Origin and Service Instructions.	Words.	At 9.15 p m.	At m.	
Vie Priority	47	From ue By F. L Pte	To By	app. IV

TO: OC N° 8th BFA Lecornet Malo

Sender's Number.	Day of Month	In reply to Number	AAA
93	12		

Unit under your comd will march tomorrow to VIÉLLÉ CHAPÉLLÉ via PACAUT – PARADIS arriving there by 9 am and take over from N° 19 BFA aaa Report arrival to me at VIÉLLÉ CHAPÉLLÉ

From ADMS Lahore Div
Place
Time 6.45 PM

* This line should be erased if not required.

"A" Form. Army Form C. 2121.

MESSAGES AND SIGNALS.

| TO | O.C. No. 8 B.F.A. | Appendix V |

Sender's Number	Day of Month	In reply to Number	
125	24		AAA

Send three amb. waggons with ten stretcher parties and an asst Surgeon under an officer to rendezvous at point on road square M21B AAA Route M20C 19B M15C ~~AA~~ ROUGECROIX LACOUTURE AAA Aid posts of Bareilly and Dehra Dun Brigades are on RUE du BACQUEROT AAA British Casualties to NO 8 B.F.A. Indian to NO 130 I.F.A via LACOUTURE and FOSSE AAA Brigades have been notified AAA

From ADMS Lahore Divn
Place
Time 6-10 pm.

Colonel
ADMS

"A" Form. Army Form C. 2121.

MESSAGES AND SIGNALS.

| TO | OC No 8 BFA | | | |

| Sender's Number | Day of Month | In reply to Number | AAA |
| 122 | 23 | | |

No 8	BFA	less	two	secs
will	march	on	relief	by
Meerut	Field	amb	No 20 BFA
on	25th	March	1915	via
R.22	FOSSE	R.9.C	R.13.B
L'EPINETTE	to	CALONNE	where
it	will	open	in	the
Small	School	and	take	in
British	Sick	of	Sirhind	Bde
aaa	remaining	two	sections	will
march	to	LE CORNET	MALO	via
FOSSE	LA CROIX	MARMUSE	PARADIS
where	they	will	remain	close
waiting	further	orders	aaa	All
sick	and	wounded	for	evacuation
on	relief	to be	transferred	to No 20 BFA

From ADMS Lahore Divn

Colonel

Sir Buvah Jeledunle

WAR DIARY

INTELLIGENCE SUMMARY.

(Erase heading not required.)

Army Form C. 2118.

Instructions regarding War Diaries and Intelligence Summaries are contained in F. S. Regs., Part II, and the Staff Manual respectively. Title pages will be prepared in manuscript.

Hour, Date, Place.	Summary of Events and Information.	Remarks and references to Appendices
April 1st 1915. CALONNE –	Returned from seven days leave to England. – Nothing Special –	S.O.C. when Gas-Gas Rem. Officers 0 0 0 0 Men. 0 2 0 3
Ap. 2–15. Same Place –	Nurse-in-chief GABRIEL A.H.Corps. – joined for duty –	Officers 0 0 0 0 Men. 3 5 0 1
Ap 3–15. Same Place –	Army Bearer Corps 20 reinforcements joined for duty. Received orders to proceed and assume the duties of A.D.M.S. of the 3rd Division – (2153 A.D.M.S. Indian Div of 3.4.15.) Major E.E. POWELL R.a.m.c. from Ambala Cav. F.d Ambulance is appointed to Command No. 8. 13 F.A. (vide supra) On his arrival Capt. J.W. LANE – R.a.m.c. left to join the Ambala Cav. F.d Amb & his Major Powell. (vide supra) Six Abdul-bearers arrived for duty from 113 Indian F.A., we had sixteen arrived same day from 113 I.F.A. The Capt. A.H.C. transferred sick from Attachment at LE CORNET MALO.	Officers 1 1 0 0 Men. 7 2 0 6 MAP FIG III

Army Form C. 2118.

WAR DIARY
or
INTELLIGENCE SUMMARY.
(Erase heading not required.)

Instructions regarding War Diaries and Intelligence Summaries are contained in F. S. Regs., Part II, and the Staff Manual respectively. Title pages will be prepared in manuscript.

Hour, Date, Place.	Summary of Events and Information.	Remarks and references to Appendices.

| April 4th 1915. CALONNE | Took over command of No 8 R.H.A. – Colonel Whalle A.M.S. received re-appointment – with No. 3rd Divison – Visits all billets and lines. Col Grayford & Capt Lahn Divison Paid us a visit this morning – Lahore Col & the Doctor – J.A. Cripe visits the Ambulance, accompanied by A.D.M.S. Lahore Div. No 39071 D.J. Walker 9th R.F.A. brought into hospital about 6 pm – Moribund – ceased breathing – Died about 5.30 pm. Day wet. Greetings. Rev? Char? Edmund? L. and from D.C.H Coy Inft. Major Fountain R.A.M.C. OFS Crowcroft O.D.I. Lodhion ch. | Adm | Inj | DIED | Rem. |
| | | Officers Men | 0 4 | 0 2 | 0 0 | 0 7 |

| April 5th – Same place | LE CORNET MALO Parade of all Europeans personnel, and Abdul Razzo this morning – Ambulance transport cleaned up – shoes etc – Kemo test viik L 113 F.H.2 – | Sick Officers Men | 0 2 | 0 3 | 0 0 | 0 6 |

| April 6th Same place | Arranging to exchange damaged water cart, cart, cook cart, to upward trolly – All divies wound dressed – hitting heavy changes hour. The cleaning Fountaine & Gt trough to continued. – Day fine & cold – Received new pattern canvas stamps | Sick Officers Men | 1 8 | 1 5 | 0 0 | 0 9 |

Army Form C. 2118.

WAR DIARY
or
INTELLIGENCE SUMMARY.
(Erase heading not required.)

Instructions regarding War Diaries and Intelligence Summaries are contained in F. S. Regs., Part II, and the Staff Manual respectively. Title pages will be prepared in manuscript.

Hour, Date, Place.	Summary of Events and Information.	Remarks and references to Appendices.
April 7th 1915. CALONNE (Wednesday)	Major R. J. Fawkes transferred sick – trench def: at LE CORNET MALO – all well – Lieut J. W. R. Shoote Rawe (Temp.) joined for duty from no 7 B.F.A. Very cloudy – Enemy intrenches – Advance slow received –	Wounded Adm. Evac. S.E.D. Rem. Sick Officers 1 1 0 0 Men. 4 7 0 6
April 8th Same place.	Transport Officer arrived early this morning and inspected Transport animals in view of A.T. carts – Saints not worn – Clothing to European & Native personnel – Col. Whale's groom left with horse etc – to Boperan to telegram received to return his men – Made at RENNINQ+ELST. One man – Pte Whelan, proceeds in 7 days leave to England from G. H. Thist. Transport out this afternoon.	Wounded Adm Evac Die Rem. Sick Officers 2 2 0 0 Men. 7 8 0 5

Army Form C. 2118.

WAR DIARY
or
INTELLIGENCE SUMMARY.
(Erase heading not required.)

Instructions regarding War Diaries and Intelligence Summaries are contained in F. S. Regs., Part II, and the Staff Manual respectively. Title pages will be prepared in manuscript.

Hour, Date, Place.	Summary of Events and Information.	Remarks and references to Appendices.
1915. April 9th CALONNE	Asst. Surg. Thana Sheet, commenced week. One temporary loss of ophthalmia. Secured from 28th Batting R.F.A. a casualties to LILLERS without delay. Asst. Surg. d'sowed kept in from attachment.	(Untraced) Sick Adm., trans. sick Rem. Officer — — 1 Men 14 16 3
April 10th Same place	Nothing special to note. Farrier had Bdr left - Lieut. Bdr. award. Arranged a new horseman 10th Fr. Tees division.	Sick 1 Officer — — 1 Men 12 6 9
April 11th Same place	Fine day. Pet inspection of future personnel. Received orders to collect kit from the Lougepoor Bde. One aeroplane came over in the morning. Sergt. Williams fined to duty.	Sick 1 Officer — — 1 Men 8 11 6
April 12th — do —	Bay horse 49 sustained a severe injury of the kick by a kick — under treatment, somedays - Destroyed by orders of V.O.	Officer — — 1 Men 13 15 4

Army Form C. 2118.

WAR DIARY
or
INTELLIGENCE SUMMARY.
(Erase heading not required.)

Instructions regarding War Diaries and Intelligence Summaries are contained in F.S. Regs., Part II, and the Staff Manual respectively. Title pages will be prepared in manuscript.

Hour, Date, Place.	Summary of Events and Information.	Remarks and references to Appendices.
April 13th CALONNE	Visit of A. Dir. M. Lahore Division. – Collecting kit from Schind, Ferozepore & Jullundur Brigades. – Two motor ambulances arrived for duty. – Lieut Surgeon Vincent D.SnO (Ammunition Column) sent sick. Evacuated in afternoon – Par à Folis. Column sent sick. Evacuated in afternoon – Par à Folis. Apps to ROUEN. = Notice of case of Enteric Inoculated. News received from PARADIS about 10 P.M. Lieut. Shôde sent out in Motor Ambulance. – Case sent on to CHOCQUES. (O.C. Station)	Sick Adm. Evac. Died Rem. Officers – – – – Men 12 11 – 5
April 14th - do -	Visited, paid out, and inspected detachment at LE CORNET MALO. – Notice of case of Measles in Lieut WARWICK'S billet. – 2,27. E.u.G. Unab BETHUNE today. Sent to A.D.M.S. Lahore Division. – Paid out personnel at No.6. B.F.A. Rue – Shorte. – Beaux & other habits personnel accidently, brown telling. – Wire asking notifying arrival of Lieut Suidair & fitter for duty. – Lieut Shôde to LILLERS with Case of Meat Fever	Sick Officers – 1 – – – 1 Men 16 -12 – – 9

Army Form C. 2118.

WAR DIARY
or
INTELLIGENCE SUMMARY.
(Erase heading not required.)

Instructions regarding War Diaries and Intelligence Summaries are contained in F. S. Regs., Part II, and the Staff Manual respectively. Title pages will be prepared in manuscript.

Hour, Date, Place.	Summary of Events and Information.	Remarks and references to Appendices.
April 15th CALONNE	Mail from Béthune & Arras — Thursday — Several cases of measles occurring in Regt. permitted leave. Corporal previously from 16th Inst. inclusive — One Officer & 1 Lorain Regt. sent to 1st Siers C.C.C. Inoculated wound in lip caused by fall from horse — Acting Adjutant Cavanagh Reinforcement in sick with measles tonight.	Sick 15th Admit Disc Rem Officers 3 3 — — Men 20 — 18 1 10
16th " "	3 more cases measles 4th Jaffray Regt — sent in this morning. One Officer (Medical) South sick from R O R F & Q - R & Co note — Stated I have been wandering from an measles — Now & 9 horse. Arrival from A.S.T.L. makes up complement.	Sick 16th Disc Rem Officers 2 2 — — Men 10 12 — 8
18th " "	Nothing special	Officers 1 1 — — Men 13 18 — 3
19th " "	Visit of DDMS. All personnel bathed at mill.	Officers 1 18 — — Men 6 7 — 2
20th " "	One Case of Ancho. Special meeting this morning. Captured by M.O.I.C.U.F. Suffering from much disturbed by bruise, who takes all further steps — Also several Medical Officers & R.R. ordered patient under the usual instructions from Ast Dr Laken Division. Officers are being taken to deal with medical keeps as directed.	Officers 3 19 — — Men 16 17 — — Officers 1 1 — — Men 21 19 — 3

Army Form C. 2118.

WAR DIARY
or
INTELLIGENCE SUMMARY.

(Erase heading not required.)

Instructions regarding War Diaries and Intelligence Summaries are contained in F. S. Regs., Part II, and the Staff Manual respectively. Title pages will be prepared in manuscript.

Hour, Date, Place.	Summary of Events and Information.	Remarks and references to Appendices.
April 2 1st CALONNE	Nothing Special - Sick Nucleus sent in detachments. 2 Officers letal Injured. Spent on 7 days' Leave to England -	Sick Officers — 1, Free — 1, Res. — 1 Men — 17, 10, 10
April 22nd " "	Visit of Officers LAHORE Division Saw two patients in hospital. Received y ea Cap more - Milk delivered in afternoon -	Sick 22nd Officers 3, 3, 1 Men 21, 26, 6
April 23rd " "	Busy during the "Sudden" so divided - Will go next week in trading to him at "Short Notice" - DCLY Press Composition takes (Appendix I) Apx I — 14 keg.	23rd Officers 8, 5, 1 Men 22, 25, 1 On Duty 2
April 24th Mond.	Marched 2-30 p.m. - Passing point LA GRAND=T=CAUT - 5-20 p.m. Long march - Arrived destination M: DECAT 1-30 a.m. following Apx III	Sick 24th Officers 1, 1, 1 Men 20, 20, 1
April 25th "		Sick 25th Officers — 1 Men — 1
OODERDOM.	Left M. DECAT 9 a.m. Arrived OODERDOM 3 p.m (about) Weather fine - Apx XI — XII	
April 26th Apx XIV	Marched to VLAMERTINGHE, a relief by 107 N.F.A. (Vide Appendix) returned to Change de POPERINGHE - At 1-50 p.m. the Braves Brincers, consisting of Capt. #9, Biggam, hich Sup. Pelt & Blaker but 5 Nursing Sisters a S. Rahim were admired out k llie village of S- JEAN - wounded Kgam, f Aum	Crossing Officers 2, 6, — Men 18, 19, —
VLAMERTINGHE	at 4.36 p.m. & Enlisted t. no to all right. Despers left m. 2, no 3	Wounded Officers 26, 24, 1 Men 288, 280, 7

Army Form C. 2118.

WAR DIARY
or
INTELLIGENCE SUMMARY.
(Erase heading not required.)

Instructions regarding War Diaries and Intelligence Summaries are contained in F. S. Regs., Part II, and the Staff Manual respectively. Title pages will be prepared in manuscript.

Hour, Date, Place.	Summary of Events and Information.	Remarks and references to Appendices.
April 26th (late) YLANERTINGHE	Canadian Field Ambulance. Many cases sent on — stay in the Church after being attended to — no evacuation during the night. Prior to their arrival.	
April 27th YLANERTINGHE (late) OUDERDOM ROAD	Shelling of this town began about 5-30 p.m. All casualties caused at Casualty Clearing Station late. Started to move out late to huts on the OUDERDOM ROAD. Arrived and moved during the night, threatening by aeroplane to move from case able to sit up, and by motor ambulance convoy for lying. Open cases — LIEUT BARCLAY and 12 men RAMC(T) stayed 2 months within fever.	27th Adm - Inoc. O.R.S. Recu — Sick Officers — 1 — — Men 44 44 — Wounded Officers — 15 — 12 4 Men 65 50 2 20 28th Sick Officers — 7 — — Men 10 9 1 Wounded Officers — 3 — — Men 92 111 1
April 28th OUDERDOM ROAD	Several casualties during night. Evacuated at 6 a.m. & 7-45 a.m. by motor. Seen & C.O. staff. — Large party assistance convoy late. Heavy shelling town & YLANERTTN G.H.E. open to-day. — LIEUT BARCLAY & men rejoined. Mr. O.C. late in this day after rendering valuable assistance — reduce fever.	

Army Form C. 2118.

WAR DIARY
or
INTELLIGENCE SUMMARY.
(Erase heading not required.)

Instructions regarding War Diaries and Intelligence Summaries are contained in F. S. Regs., Part II, and the Staff Manual respectively. Title pages will be prepared in manuscript.

Hour, Date, Place.	Summary of Events and Information.	Remarks and references to Appendices.
April 29th OUDERDOM ROAD	Not taking in Casualties to-day – Noticed 1 move to OUDERDOM at 6 p.m. Arrived about 9 p.m. – Encamped in a field 200 yards E. of main road – S. end of village – Much artillery fire – Otherwise quiet night.	29th April Sick Adm. Evac. Died Reman. Officers – – – 1 Men – – – 1
April 30th RENNINGHELST.	Orders 1st Moves this morning of 6.0 a.m. to RENNINGHELST. & came outside town until 8 a.m. – Awaiting further orders – Arrived 10.30 – Issued wire 1st & 9th & numerous aircraft. Quiet day – Later 70th LAHORE Div. arrived & will relieve 1st Division where we were for the present. App. XV = 3rd	30th April Sick Officers – – – 1 Men – – – 1

Alfred Capt. Reeve
O. C. No. 9. F.a.

App 1.

Copy of a letter from D.G. M.S. G.H.Q. No P 937/97
31-3-15.

Major E. E. Powell R.A.M.C. Ambala Cavalry Field Ambulance is appointed to command No 8 British Field Ambulance, Lahore Division, & should join accordingly forthwith.

A regular R.A.M.C. officer will be detailed from the latter unit for duty with Ambala Cavalry Field Ambulance.

No 920 MED 1st Ind. Cav. Dn.
  1-4-15.

The O.C. Ambala C. F. A.

For necessary action. Please report date of this officer's departure.

Sd. G. D. Hunter Col.
True copy [signature] A.D.M.S 1st I.C.D.
5-4-15. Major R.A.M.C.
  O.C. No 8. B F Amb

App. 11

Copy of a letter from D.D.M.S. G.H.Q. No D 937 of 31-3-15.

Major E. E. Powell R.A.M.C. Ambala Cavalry Field Ambulance is appointed to command No 8 British Field Ambulance, Lahore Division, & should join accordingly forthwith.

A regular R.A.M.C. officer will be detailed from the latter unit for duty with Ambala Cavalry Field Ambulance.

No 920 MED   1st Ind. Cav. Dn.
                       1.4.15.

The O.C. Ambala C.F.A.
For necessary action. Please report date of this officer's departure.

                       Sd. G. D. Hunter Col.
True Copy   A.D.M.S. 1st I.C.D.
5.4.15.   Major R.A.M.C.
           O.C. No 8 B F Amb

Extract from Ambala Cavalry Fd Ambulance
Orders by Lieut Colonel A.E. Berry I.M.S.
Commanding of 2-4-1915.

208

Under instructions received from ADMS 1st
Indian Cavalry Division Major E.E. Powell
R.A.M.C. is directed to proceed forthwith, to take
Command of No 8. British Field Ambulance
Lahore Division.

Sd/ A. E. Berry.
Lt Colonel I. M. S.
Comdg Amb Cav. Fd. Amb

True Extract.

5-4.15.

Major R.A.M.C
O.C. No 8. B. F Amb.

"C" Form (Duplicate).   Army Form C. 2123.
            MESSAGES AND SIGNALS.   No. of Message

	Charges to Pay.	Office Stamp.
Service Instructions.	£ s. d. ✓	14-4 Z 11

Handed in at the _____ Office, at _____ .m. Received here at _____ .m.

TO OC NO 8 B F H.
    CALONNE

Sender's Number.	Day of Month.	In reply to Number.	AAA
2370	14		

Send Motor Ambulance to
LILLERS for Lieut N.T
Sinclair R.A.M.C arrived today
& posted to Your
Unit.

FROM   A. DMS
PLACE Lahore Division
TIME

"C" Form (Duplicate).
MESSAGES AND SIGNALS.

Army Form C. 2123.
No. of Message ____

Charges to Pay.
£ s. d.

Office Stamp.

Service Instructions.

Handed in at the _____ Office, at _____ .m. Received here at _____ .m.

TO O.C. No 8 B.F.A. CALONNE

Sender's Number.	Day of Month.	In reply to Number.	AAA
183	23		
In	the	Event	of
Sudden	move	Brigades	and
Divl	troops	directed	to
send	British	sick	to
L'EPINETTE	Indian	sick	to
PARADIS	AAA	Until	move
is	ordered	sick	as
before	to	CALONNE	

FROM A.D.M.S Lahore Division
PLACE
TIME

"C" Form (Duplicate).
Army Form C. 2123.
MESSAGES AND SIGNALS.

Charges to Pay.

Service Instructions.

Handed in at the _____ Office, at _____ m. Received here at _____ m.

TO: O.C. No. 8 B.F.A. CALONNE.

Sender's Number.	Day of Month.	In reply to Number.	AAA
184	24.		
Be	prepared	to	move
at	short	notice AAA	Waggons
to	be	packed AAA	Evacuate
sick	in	unit AAA	Further
cases	of	sickness	to be
sent	British	to	L'EPINETTE
Indian	to	PARADIS	

FROM: A.D.M.S. Lahore Division
PLACE:
TIME: 10.25 A.M.

"A" Form
Army Form C. 2121.

MESSAGES AND SIGNALS.

Prefix	Code	m.	Words	Charge		This message is on a/c of:	Recd. at	m.
Office of Origin and Service Instructions			Sent				Date	
			At	m.		**VII** Service.	From	
			To				By	
			By			(Signature of "Franking Officer.")		

TO O.C. No 8 B.F.A CALONNE

Sender's Number	Day of Month	In reply to Number	
186	24		AAA

Your unit will march for KRUIX TRAELE and south of MT. DESCAT starting point LE GRAND PACAUT for leading field ambulance 3.20 pm to day AAA Order of march in rear of 18th Bde R.F.A No 8 B.F.A No 113 I.F.A No 112 I.F.A No 7 B.F.A No 111 I.F.A AAA Motor Ambulances to proceed in rear of Divl Ammn Column and should leave LE GRAND PACAUT at 4.15 pm and rejoin units at destination AAA Officer should be sent ahead to meet C.R.A for billeting purposes. AAA No 113 I.F.A to open on arrival and be prepared

From
Place
Time

The above may be forwarded as now corrected.   (Z)

Censor.   Signature of Addressor or person authorized to telegraph in his name
* This line should be erased if not required.

"A" Form.
Army Form C. 2121.

MESSAGES AND SIGNALS.

No. of Message

Prefix	Code	m.	Word-	Charge	This message is on a/c of:	Recd. at	m.
Office of Origin and Service Instructions.			Sent			Date	
			At	m.	Service.	From	
			To				
			By		(Signature of "Franking Officer.")	By	

TO (2)

| * | Sender's Number | Day of Month | In reply to Number | AAA |

to take m sick AAA
Report arrival to Divl Hd Qrs
at BOESCHEPE AAA Reference HAZEBROUCK
map 5A 1/100,000 AAA Route
VERTERUE LA RUE DU BOIS VIEX BERQUIN
STRAZEELE FLETRE

From ADMS Lahore Division
Place
Time 1.30 pm

The above may be forwarded as now corrected.   (Z)

Censor. Signature of Addressor or person authorised to telegraph in his name
* This line should be erased if not required.

"A" Form.
MESSAGES AND SIGNALS.
Army Form No. of Message ____

| Prefix ___ Code ___ m. | Words | Charge | This message is on a/c of: | Recd. at ___ m. |
| Office of Origin ___ Service Instructions ___ | Sent At ___ m. To ___ By ___ | | **IX** Service. (Signature of "Franking Officer.") | Date ___ From ___ By ___ |

TO { Field Ambulance

| Sender's Number | Day of Month | In reply to Number | AAA |
| G 638 | 24 | | |

British sick to No 8 B.F.A. at MT. DESCATS AAA Indian sick to No 113 I.F.A. in school at GODEWAERSVELDE

From: Lahore Div. Art.
Place:
Time: 11.45 pm

The above may be forwarded as now corrected.   (Z)
Censor. Signature of Addresser or person authorised to telegraph in his name
* This line should be erased if not required.
158 S.B. Ltd. Wt. W5673/619—50,000. 10/14. Forms C2121/10.

"A" Form. Army Form C. 2121.

MESSAGES AND SIGNALS.

Prefix	Code	m.	Words	Charge	This message is on a/c of:	Recd. at	m.
Office of Origin and Service Instructions.			Sent At ___ m. To ___ By ___		Service. (Signature of "Franking Officer.")	Date ___ From ___ By ___	

TO O.C. No 8 B.F.H.

Sender's Number	Day of Month	In reply to Number	AAA
188	24		

Billet tonight in School below MONASTERY and open tomorrow morning for reception of British sick of Divn AAA Location of units AAA Jullundur Bde and 11th Bde R.F.A. BOESCHAPE AAA Sirhind Bde and 18th Bde RFA BERTHEM AAA Ferozepore Bde and 5th Bde RFA GODE WAERSVELDE AAA Motor Ambulances to be used for BOESCHAPE and BERTHEM AAA Sick to be collected at 9 AM

From ADMS Lahore Divn

"C" Form (Original). Army Form C. 2123

MESSAGES AND SIGNALS.

TO: Field Ambulance

Sender's Number: G.636
Day of Month: 24.

Division will march tomorrow at about 7 A.M. AAA Definite orders follow

FROM: Lahore Divl. Art:
PLACE:
TIME: 11-30 pm

"A" Form.   Army Form C. 2121.

MESSAGES AND SIGNALS.   No. of Message

Prefix	Code	m.	Words	Charge			Recd. at	m.
Office of Origin and Service Instructions.					This message is on a/c of:		Date	
			Sent		**X II**		From	
			At	m.		Service.		
			To				By	
			By		(Signature of "Franking Officer.")			

TO   O.C. No 8 B.F.A.

Sender's Number	Day of Month	In reply to Number	
192	24		AAA

Your unit will march tomorrow to HUTMUNTS NE of OUDERDOM field ambulance passing the starting point Road junction just NORTH of the R in MT KOKEREELE commencing 10.40 AM AAA Order of march No 8 BFA No 113 IFA No 112 IFA No 7 BFA and No 111 IFA AAA the leading field Ambulance No 8 BFA following the 15th Lancers AAA Route HEKSKEM RENINGHELST road along north bank of river RENINGHELST road junction quarter mile north of the in OUDERDOM AAA Billeting Officer from each field Amb to meet a Dvr Staff Officer at the commencement of the

From			
Place			
Time			

The above may be forwarded as now corrected.   (Z)

Censor.   Signature of Addressor or person authorised to telegraph in his name

* This line should be erased if not required.

"A" Form.   Army Form C. 2121.
MESSAGES AND SIGNALS.   No. of Message

Prefix	Code	m.	Words	Charge			Recd. at	m.
Office of Origin and Service Instructions.		Sent			This message is on a/c of:		Date	
		At	m.			Service.	From	
		To					By	
		By			(Signature of "Franking Officer.")			

TO {

Sender's Number	Day of Month	In reply to Number	AAA
Starts	at	8:30 AM AAA	One
Section	No 8 B.F.A	and one Section	No 113 I.F.A
to	stand	fast till sick	Evacuated
and	wait	further orders.	AAA
Reference	Map	HAZEBROUCK 1/100,000	AAA
Reports	to	GODEWAERSVELDE till	8.30 AM
25th	and	after 11 am.	at
OUDERDOM AAA	Refilling	point	on
25th	FLETRE 8 AM AAA	All	Empty
Supply	wagons	to be S. of a	line
drawn	E and W.	through	LE COQ-de-
PAILLE	about	one mile	NORTH
of	FLETRE	at 9 A.M	AAA
Supply	wagons	will approach	FLETRE
from	the	north	VIA METREM
H	of FONTAINEHOUCK	to cross road	half

From			
Place			
Time			

The above may be forwarded as now corrected. (Z)

Censor. Signature of Addressor or person authorised to telegraph in his name
* This line should be erased if not required.

"A" Form. Army Form C. 2121.

MESSAGES AND SIGNALS.   No. of Message

Prefix	Code	m.	Words	Charge	This message is on a/c of:	Recd. at	m.
Office of Origin and Service Instructions.		Sent				Date	
		At		m.	Service.	From	
		To				By	
		By			(Signature of "Franking Officer.")		

TO — 3

| * | Sender's Number | Day of Month | In reply to Number | AAA |

mile	north	west	of	ST JANS CAPPEL
BERTHEN	MT. KOKEREELE		thence	follow
route	of	Division	north	of
MT KOKEREELE	and	N	of	RENINGHELST
river	rendezvous	for	supply	wagons
road	junction	quarter	mile	W. of the
O. of	OUDERDOM	AAA	field	Ambulances
belong	to	Divl	Troops	refilling
group	AAA	Motor	Ambulances	to
visit	areas	of	troops	and
collect	all	sick	after	10 A.M.

From ADMS Lahore Divn
Place
Time 12 pm

The above may be forwarded as now corrected. (Z)

Censor. Signature of Addressor or person authorised to telegraph in his name

* This line should be erased if not required.

"C" Form (Duplicate). Army Form C. 2123.
MESSAGES AND SIGNALS.   No. of Message

Charges to Pay. Office Stamp.
£ s. d
XIII

Service Instructions.

Handed in at the _____ Office, at _____ .m. Received here at _____ .m.

TO O.C. No. 8 BFA

Sender's Number.	Day of Month.	In reply to Number.	AAA
197	25		
Collect	sick	this	evening
by	motor	Ambulances	AAA
Troops	of	Divn	are
in	huts	on	ODERDUM
VLAMERTINGHE	road	about	1½
miles	from	ODERDUM	

FROM A.D.M.S Lahore Divn
PLACE
TIME

"C" Form (Duplicate). Army Form C. 2123.
MESSAGES AND SIGNALS.

XIV

Service Instructions.

Handed in at the _____ Office, at _____ .m. Received here at _____ .m.

TO: O.C. NO 8 B.F.A ODERDOM

Sender's Number.	Day of Month.	In reply to Number.	AAA
201	26		
On	relief	by	No 7 B.F.A
your	unit	will	march
this	morning	to	VLAMERTINGHE
and	open	there	for
reception	of	casualties	AAA
Bearer	Divn	to be	ready
to	form	Advanced	dressing
Station	on	receipt	of
further	orders	AAA	Motor
Ambulance	Waggons	accompany	you
AAA	An	Officer	from
your	Unit	should	be
detailed	forthwith	to	proceed

FROM
PLACE
TIME

"C ~~form~~ (Original). Army Form C. 2123
MESSAGES AND SIGNALS. No. of Message _____

Prefix	Code	Words	Received	Sent, or sent out	Office Stamp.
	£ s. d.		From_____	At_____ m.	
Charges to collect			By_____	To_____	
Service Instructions.				By_____	

Handed in at the _____ Office, at _____ .m. Received here at _____ .m.

TO _____ (2) _____

*Sender's Number.	Day of Month.	In reply to Number.	AAA
to	VLAMERTINGHE	and	reserve
accomodation	in	that	place
for	reception	of	casualties
AAA	Instructions	should	be
left	for	your	detached
Section	on	arrival	to
join	you	at	VLAMERTINGHE
forthwith.			

FROM A.D.M.S. Lahore Divn
PLACE
TIME 5-10 A.M.

* This line should be erased if not required.

"C" F... (Original). Army Form C. 2123
MESSAGES AND SIGNALS.

Prefix	Code	Words	Received	Sent, or sent out	Office Stamp.
		£ s. d.	From	At m.	
Charges to collect			By	To	XV
Service Instructions.				By	

Handed in at the _____ Office, at _____ .m. Received here at _____ .m.

TO O C NO. 8. B.F.A.

*Sender's Number.	Day of Month.	In reply to Number.	AAA
213	30		

Your unit to move to the north of RENINGHELST moving by route to the E. of GROTEBECKE and be clear of RENINGHELST by 11 am AAA Bivouacing till about 5pm AAA Your unit will march this evening with Lahore Divn less Sirhind Bde to billets in area BURTEN (exclusive) KRUISTRAETES - CAESTRE (exclusive) FLETRE METEREN St JANS CAPPEL (exclusive) and a billeting officer should meet

FROM
PLACE
TIME

*This line should be erased if not required.

"C" Form (Original). Army Form C. 2123
MESSAGES AND SIGNALS.   No. of Message

Prefix	Code	Words	Received	Sent, or sent out	Office Stamp.
	£ s. d.		From	At m.	
Charges to collect			By	To	
Service Instructions.				By	

Handed in at the _____ Office, at _____ .m. Received here at _____ .m.

TO (2)

*Sender's Number.	Day of Month.	In reply to Number.	AAA

The D.A.A.G. at RENINGHELST cross road at 10 A.M. AAA On arrival at new area you will open for reception and collection of Sick from Jullundur and Ferozepore Bdes and 15th Lancers position of which will be notified hereafter. AAA Refilling point to day will be as yesterday. AAA A look out to be kept on the road for all Sick and stragglers falling out on the march and these should be collected as far as possible. AAA Report arrival to Divl H. Qrs. position of which will be notified later

FROM   ADMS Lahore Divn.
PLACE
TIME   8.15 A.M.

*This line should be erased if not required.

"C" Form (Original).   Army Form C. 2123
MESSAGES AND SIGNALS.   No. of Message _____

	Code ___ Words ___	Received	Sent, or sent out	Office Stamp.
	£ s. d.	From ___	At ___ m.	
Charges to collect		By ___	To ___	XVI
Service Instructions.			By ___	

Handed in at the _____ Office, at _____ m. Received here at _____ m.

TO O.C. N° 8 B.F.A.

*Sender's Number.	Day of Month.	In reply to Number.	AAA
H.Q. 286	30		
Ref.	operation	order	No 1
Troops	of	LAHORE	DIV.
now	in	bivouac	N.W
of	the	GROOTE BECKE	will
stand	fast	until	further
orders	DIV. H°Qrs	remains	at
POPERINGHE			

FROM LAHORE DIVN
PLACE
TIME 3.45 p.m.

*This line should be erased if not required.

No. 8. M.J.A.

COMMITTEE FOR THE
MEDICAL HISTORY OF THE WAR
4 NOV 1919

Army Form C. 2118.

WAR DIARY
or
INTELLIGENCE SUMMARY.

(Erase heading not required.)

No 8. B.F.Q. May 1915.

Instructions regarding War Diaries and Intelligence Summaries are contained in F.S. Regs., Part II, and the Staff Manual respectively. Title pages will be prepared in manuscript.

Hour, Date, Place.	Summary of Events and Information.	Remarks and references to Appendices.
May 1st PENNINGHELST – BOESCHEPE	This morning halted march to BOESCHEPE at 4 p.m. following No 112 I.E.A. – arrived 6.30 p.m. – Recruits average from Reserve. & arrange for a place to billet in each bivouac – App I	May 1st Sick - - - Admis Evac. Res. Rem Officers - - - Men 2 - 3
May 2nd BOESCHEPE	Established M.D. keeping Station at "Windmill Farm". Phu Case steamed to C.C. Station BAILLEUL. All cases evacuated later and despatch Station Church trays & ??? & ??? & Meals washed Latrines & Washed at 7.30. Followed the Sect Ammunition Column round to MORTIER via BAILLEUL about midnight – halted in round late in new camp & go to CALONNE via old filter. Left at 4.30 a.m. via ESTAIRES & MERVILLE arriving 9-10 a.m. App II – III	May 2nd Sick - - - Officers - 14 - 17 - Men - - -
May 3rd CALONNE		May 3rd Sick - - - Officers 2. 0. 0. 2 Men - - -
May 4th Same place.	Nothing particular to note. Setts billets.	May 4th Sick - - - Officers 1 1 - - Men 9 5 - 6

Army Form C. 2118.

WAR DIARY
or
INTELLIGENCE SUMMARY.

No 8. B. F. A. — May 1915.

(Erase heading not required.)

Instructions regarding War Diaries and Intelligence Summaries are contained in F.S. Regs., Part II, and the Staff Manual respectively. Title pages will be prepared in manuscript.

Hour, Date, Place.	Summary of Events and Information.	Remarks and references to Appendices.
May 5th — CALONNE	Nothing to report — Intelligence Report attached close —	May 5th Sick Adm. was DIED Rem. Officers 3 - 2 - 1 Men. 29 - 35 - - May 6th Sick Adm was DIED Rem. Gought Officers 1 1 - - 1 Men 13 13 - - -
May 6th — CALONNE	Received orders (App IV) to march tonight to HQ of SIRHIND BDE via LESTREM to join no R.16.c. (ref. map FRANCE, 1/40,000 BETHUNE) We left about 9-45 p.m. and arrived at 1 a.m. R. 5-16 — without incident. Information given around was telegraphed at once to H.Q.d LAHORE DIVISION, and Reception bivouac prepared for sick & wounded (horse) The Lahore Division was lifted off, and held in district reserve to serve.	
May 4th R.16.c. (map FRANCE 1/40000 BETHUNE.)	Night passed quietly — Up at 4.30 am, and out shortly after, seeing after the Watti Supper, Latrine arrangement to the vicinity etc. Two officers — Capt O'GORDON RAWE, and Lieut B.P.NOBLE joined for duty — Yesterday at CALONNE. Two more is joining today. Visit of A.D.M.S. LAHORE DIV. this morning — Medical duties of Lahore division for tonight.	

Gulab Singh & Sons, Calcutta — No. 22 Army C. — 5.8.14 — 1.07.000.

Army Form C. 2118.

WAR DIARY
or
INTELLIGENCE SUMMARY.

No 8. B.F.A. — May 1915

(Erase heading not required.)

Instructions regarding War Diaries and Intelligence Summaries are contained in F.S. Regs., Part II, and the Staff Manual respectively. Title pages will be prepared in manuscript.

Hour, Date, Place.	Summary of Events and Information.	Remarks and references to Appendices.
May 7th R.16.C. (camp)	Notes of question taken. Orders for line of communication units. Order from A.D.M.S. to collect Book of FEROZEPORE BRIG Hdq of Brigade M.I.D. **App V. Ip.**	
May 8th Same place	Obliged to go sick with Laryngitis – handed over command to Capt O'Riordan R.A.M.C.	Admissions Wounded 1 B.R. 1 O.R.B. Sick 1 B.R. 2 O.R.B. Evacuated 1 B.R. sick
6 pm App VI	S.Singh Major R.A.M.C. took over command of unit. (reference A.D.M.S. Lahore Division orders attached) at 6 pm. Received orders from A.D.M.S. at 6.12 pm to send out full Bearer Division to form a combined dressing Station with Bearer Division of No 112 I.F.A. at M27.D.11. by 12 midnight. Orders issued to Capt. O'Riordan R.A.M.C. to move out. The bearer division at 10.30 pm. The bivouac in the field 150 yds North of M27.D.11. Tonga ambulances to accompany his division to pick them behind house at M24.A.11. Hospital Stretcher bearers are on South side of the Road at that point. No road of Jullunder Brigade to be cleared at midnight. Bearer Division sent on at Dressing Station till further orders are out. Ambulance wagons to follow Route laid down in Traffic kept. (Vide Appendix No **VII**) altered. Extra blankets. Dressings & bandages sent out with Bearer Division. Bearer Division marched out at 11.5 pm.	A.Hukhll Capt R.A.M.C

Army Form C. 2118.

WAR DIARY
or
INTELLIGENCE SUMMARY.

No 9. B.F.A. May 1915.

(Erase heading not required.)

Hour, Date, Place.	Summary of Events and Information.	Remarks and references to Appendices.
R.16.c. 9/5/15	Bearer Division arrived at M.27.D.1.1. at 12.15am formed a combined dressing station with No 112 F.A. Poulson & Regimental Aid Posts 1/5 before Brigade. CONNAUGHT RANGERS M.27.D.4.8. South side of Road 1/4 LONDON M.27.D. 6.10 North of Farm ESTAIRES - LA BASSÉE Road JULLUNDUR BRIGADE 1st MANCHESTER REG. M line between 27.D.-28.C at beginning of Tramway. 4 SUFFOLKS M.34.A. 4.4 cross roads 7 h am ESTAIRES - LA BASSÉE Aid posts were cleared & stretcher parts were left at the aid posts cases collected were dressed & sent to 2nd Division Bearer division personnel were accommodated in informed huts before Artillery bombardment commenced. After the bombardment aid posts & huts retained - Stretcher bearers returned to the Aid Post. & wounded cases & the Dressing Station - Stretcher Squads were released at 4.30pm. Capt. O'Riordan was released by Capt. Read Kane at 9.30pm. 2nd Division would accommodate 150 cases - 80 lying & 70 sitting cases. Separate tents used for Head. Abdominal - lung & severe fracture cases. Cases Evacuated by No VII Convoy at 10.30 am 3 pm. 4.30pm. Field Ambulance held by Surgeon General Macpherson - Col Pike Col Seyfort. Tel Col Sloan - D.M.S. 1st Army - D.D.M.S. I.A.C. A.D.M.S LAHORE DIVISION & D.A.D.M.S LAHORE DIVISION treatin & full team.	Admissions wounded 8 officers 63 ORs Sick — 1 OR Evacuated wounded 4 officers 33 ORs Sick 3 ORs

Army Form C. 2118.

WAR DIARY
or
INTELLIGENCE SUMMARY.
(Erase heading not required.)

Instructions regarding War Diaries and Intelligence Summaries are contained in F.S. Regs., Part II, and the Staff Manual respectively. Title pages will be prepared in manuscript.

No 8. B.F.A. May 1915.

Hour, Date, Place.	Summary of Events and Information.	Remarks and references to Appendices.
R.16.c. 10-5-15.	Bearer Division is still at advanced Dressing Station. Few wounded are being cut back to the Field Dressing. Motor Convoy cleared the Hospital by 1pm. Lieut B.B. NOBLE R.A.M.C was cut out at 9pm to relieve Lieut WARWICK R.A.M.C. 4th Class Bearer Surgeon. R.T.M. HAYTER I.S.M.D. joined out for temporary duty. Weather bright & warm. Jflm	Admissions Wounded off. nil O.R.B 22 Evacuated 5 45 Sick 1
R.16.c. 11-5-15.	Received orders at 11-15 am. from A.D.M.S. LAHORE Division to withdraw Dressing Station. Hottest casualties from Brigades at night, also Officer rode attached. 10 VIII Received order from A.D.M.S. Lahore Division at 3-4.5pm to collect Sick of Division (vide officer slightly wounded from Volunteer Bn. attached IX attached) 4th Class Casual Surgeon R.T.M. HAYTER I.S.M.D. detailed for duty with 13 Batt R.F.A 3pm Lahore Division sent 12-45pm. Bearer Division rejoined Lahore Division at 3-30 pm. Weather bright & warm. Jflm	Admissions Wounded off. nil O.R.B 3 Evacuated nil 8 Sick nil 1 Evacuated nil remaining one
R.16.c. 12-5-15.	Collected Sick from FEROZEPORE & SIRHIND BRIGADES. 2 Wagons cut out at 10am. 1 Coast Brigade. 2 wagons out at 9am. 16 R.F.A. H.D. 3 kr. 16 R.A.M.C. orderlies arrived from MERVILLE D.D.M.S. I.A.C. halted him at 11am. and took of JULLUNDER BRIG cleared at 10.15 km. 2 wounded brought in. Weather bright & warm. Jflm	Admissions Wounded off. nil O.R.B 3 Evacuated nil 12 Sick nil 3 Evacuated nil

WAR DIARY
or
INTELLIGENCE SUMMARY. 8 B.F.A.   MAY 1915

Army Form C. 2118.

(Erase heading not required.)

Instructions regarding War Diaries and Intelligence Summaries are contained in F.S. Regs., Part II, and the Staff Manual respectively. Title pages will be prepared in manuscript.

Hour, Date, Place.	Summary of Events and Information.	Remarks and references to Appendices
R 16 c. 13-5-15-	Capt. W. H. O'RIORDAN - RAMC reported No. 7 B.F.A. under orders from A.D.M.S. Lahore Division. Special orders issued re his B Officers. Two Officers admitted suffering from Measles. Two cases Influenza B Case admitted to hospital. No motor Convoy arrived. Evacuated Sick Wounded. Ad posts of JULLUNDUR BRIG cleared of Sick Wounded. Sick cleared from FEROZEPORE & SIRHIND BRIG's Weather dull cold rainy. Was difficult to obtain in this neighbourhood. JH.	Admissions OR.B. Officers 4 kil 24 Wounded Sick 4 Evacuated Nil
R 16 c. 14-5-15	Motor convoy cleared the unit at 2 p.m. 4 dental cases evacuated by A.D.M.S. & evacuated to No. 4 C.C.S. LILLERS under instructions from A.D.M.S. Received Verbal orders from D.A.D.M.S. to send out full Bearer Division to M.2. Y.d. 11. Bearer Division to reach that spot at 9 p.m. Later instructions from D.A.D.M.S. cancelled at 4 pm. Weather dull and damp. JH	Admissions OR.B. Officers 12 kil 9 Wounded Evacuated 3 Sick 19 Evacuated 5 Case to Invalid by LILLERS 31
R 16 c. 15-5-15-	One patient died in hospital from wounds was buried in VIELLE CHAPELLE. No 2 motor convoy evacuated cases at 12 noon. 7.25 p.m. Received orders from A.D.M.S. Lahore Division to send out full Bearer Division to form a Collecting Dressing Station with Bearer Division of No. 112 J.F.A. at M.24.d.11. by 9.30 p.m. Orders issued to hand WARWICK R.A.M.C. to command Bearer Division & made it out at 8.30 p.m. to comply the A.D.M.S. orders. Vide Appdx. Not attached. Bearer Division accompanied by 2 motor ambulance cars was expected by me Finished out at Enzo.	Admissions OR.B. Officers 15 kil 9 Wounded Evacuated 2 Sick 11 Evacuated 3 Case to Invalid by LILLERS 13.

Army Form C. 2118.

WAR DIARY
or
INTELLIGENCE SUMMARY.

No 8 B.F.A. - May 1915

(Erase heading not required.)

Instructions regarding War Diaries and Intelligence Summaries are contained in F. S. Regs., Part II, and the Staff Manual respectively. Title pages will be prepared in manuscript.

Hour, Date, Place.	Summary of Events and Information.	Remarks and references to Appendices
R 16 c 15-5-15-	Bearer Division from No 4 B.F.A. & 113 I.F.A. arrived at 9.20 p.m. Report of wounded to be continued until stopped by 6 am 12 noon & 9 pm to be continued until stopped by order of D.M.S. 1st Army. Weather bright mild after.	
R 16 c 16-5-15-	12-15 am another motor ambulance wagon called for by O.C. Bearer Division. D.D.M.S. 1 A.C. visited unit at 9 am. A.D.M.S. at 10-30 am. Lucknow field dressing station with A.D.M.S. at 11 am. Hospital cleared at 12 noon by No 2 M.A.C. One man died in hospital from wounds. 12 men of R.A.M.C. attached by A.D.M.S. & 9 rmn. Their respective Brigades for water duty. Took in civil sight as no cases are coming in from the dressing station. Reports sent to A.D.M.S. at 6 am 12 noon 7-9 pm. Received orders from A.D.M.S. to collect service of SIRHIND BRIGADE at 9-30 am from X 46.8.3 on 17-5-15. Weather bright warm after.	admissions wounded off. 1 wounded O.R. 7 evacuated O.R. 16 sick 2 2 evacuated 1 4 Sent to convalescent by LILLERS. Dead men buried in VIEILLE CHAPELLE 4
R 16 c 17-5-15-	D.D.M.S. 1 A.C. visited unit at 9 am. Sick from SIRHIND Brig. collected at 9.30 through to hospital at 11 am. One man (died of wounds received in action) at 5 am. Sick throughout cleared by No 2 M.A.C. at 12 noon. A.D.M.S. unsefield visit at 10 am unpacked one tooth case - which he ordered to be evacuated to LILLERS. Bearer division still at dressing station. Work bright - weather still warm after.	admissions wounded off. ORs 15 evacuated off. 5 sick 20 evacuated 2 14 sent to LILLERS 3

Gulab Singh & Sons, Calcutta—No. 22 Army C.—5-8-14—1,07,000.

Army Form C. 2118.

WAR DIARY
or
INTELLIGENCE SUMMARY.

(Erase heading not required.)

No 9. B.F.A.   May 19/15.

Instructions regarding War Diaries and Intelligence Summaries are contained in F. S. Regs., Part II, and the Staff Manual respectively. Title pages will be prepared in manuscript.

Hour, Date, Place.	Summary of Events and Information.	Remarks and references to Appendices
R 16 C 18-5-15	D.D.M.S. visited unit 9am. A.D.M.S. at 10am. Received orders from A.D.M.S. 10-20 am to recall Bearer Division - also 1 sub Section under an Asst Surgeon and one motor Ambulance. Relief Bte arranged for. Highly Collection Bgrounded at 9.30 pm. (Vide Appdx. XIII attached) Issued order to OC Bearer Division at 10-10. (Vide Appd to XIV) attached No 2 M.A.C. cleared Sick + wounded at 11.45 am. - Two hand cases to be retained in Hospital for ADMS's inspection. Received orders from A.D.M.S. (7-45 pm.) that unit must move at once to Square R. 13 D. - wounded to be transferred to No Y.B.F.A. unit to remain closed until further orders - motor cars to be transferred to No Y.B.F.A. (Vide Appd to No XV) attached. Above order cancelled at 8-10 pm. A.D.M.S. order (vide appendix XVI attached) Order received at 8-50 pm to collect Sick (Vide appendix XVII). JULLUNDUR BRIG. from 19-5-15. Hdq BRIG M.I.D. weather dull. 7pm.	admissions wounded officers 1 ORB Evacuated 1 21 Sick 1 12 Evacuated 1 8 to Con absent 64 11 LILLERS 6
R 16 C 19-5-15	D.D.M.S. visited unit at 9am. A.D.M.S. at 10 am Sick Collected from JULLUNDUR BRIG. at 9.30. Two hand cases to be evacuated. No 2 M.A.C. cleared unit at 12-5 pm. Bearer Subdivision Attached by B sub division - highly collection Bgrounded as usual FEROZEPORE BRIG. in the Trinches weather Dull 7pm.	admissions wounded officers ORB hit 3 Evacuated 21 hit 5 Sick Evacuated hit 8 Evd to LILLERS hit today.

Army Form C. 2118.

WAR DIARY
or
INTELLIGENCE SUMMARY.

No 8 B.F.A.

May 1915

(Erase heading not required.)

Instructions regarding War Diaries and Intelligence Summaries are contained in F. S. Regs., Part II, and the Staff Manual respectively. Title pages will be prepared in manuscript.

Hour, Date, Place.	Summary of Events and Information.	Remarks and references to Appendices
R. 16 c. 20-5-15	D.D.M.S. held unit at 9am. A.D.M.S. at 10am. Sick collected from JULLUNDUR BRIG at 9.30 am. 162.M.A.C. cleared the unit at 12 noon. One man 12th Worces. Li. Reg. died in the Field Ambulance. One stuck Interpreter Soldier. 9. LANCE 16 INF joined for duty. 3-30 pm. Received orders from A.D.M.S. to 29oin. No. 7 B.F.A on relief by MAJOR GIBSON R.A.M.C. 9.30 pm. Received instruction from A.D.M.S. to personally superintend the arrangements necessary for an advanced Dressing Station — Lahore Division — at M27D54 advanced Dressing Station to be a combined one for British & Indian Sick & Wounded. (vide attend XVIII) Weather bright & warm.	Admissions ORB Wounded Officers 8 hd 3 Evacuated — One man died from wounds Sick 1 15— Evacuated hd 8 Remaining 1 9
R. 16 c. 21-5-15	D.D.M.S. visited unit at 9am. D.A.D.M.S. visited unit at 11am. & accompanied me to advanced Dressing Station. A.D.M.S. visited unit at 3pm. inspected & took type cases — all to be evacuated. Visited dressing Station at 3-30pm. Temporarily arrangements for its opening then reported to the A.D.M.S. that arrangements made from necessary — failing that Shelters should be erected and cleared by No 2 tarpaulins. M.A.C. at 12 noon. Dead failed buried in NEUVE CHAPELLE. Rainy & bright intervals. After.	Admissions ORB Wounded Officers 4 hd 9 Evacuated hd 18 Sick hd 13 Evacuated

Army Form C. 2118.

WAR DIARY
or
INTELLIGENCE SUMMARY.

No 8 B.F.A.

May 1915

(Erase heading not required.)

Instructions regarding War Diaries and Intelligence Summaries are contained in F. S. Regs., Part II, and the Staff Manual respectively. Title pages will be prepared in manuscript.

Hour, Date, Place.	Summary of Events and Information.	Remarks and references to Appendices
R 16 c. 22-5-15.	D.D.M.S. visited the unit at 9am. Enfield dressing Station at 2am everything in good order. 10 am Medical Board held on two Warrant officers - for recurrent communism. 11 am Enfield Dressing Station and R tot H.A. HIME R.A.M.C. A.D.M.S. visited dressing station while we were there. Dressing Station is divided into two parts one for British the other for Indians - each with its own dressing room, 1 accommodation for officers - lying cases divided into hay there trades. Head Pakistan for Kistans. Latrines - Urinals - Refuse pits etc for Indians & British. A.D.M.S. was satisfied & returned with the tent Division. For around two cases of Dental Caries. D.A.D.M.S. & D.D.M.S. visited the unit in the Evening. Work Slight - Weather warm Stoped Afth. No 2 hoal closed the unit at 12 noon 73.30 pm.	Admissions O.R.B officers 1 13 wounded Evacuated 1 6. Sick 2 16 Evacuated 3 17
R 16 c. 23-5-15.	D.D.M.S. visited unit at 9.45 am. Enfield M.D Root One man was brought in dead by Ambulance Wagon. 11am held advanced dressing Station. No 2 M.A.C. cleared unit at 12 noon & 6.30pm. Handed over command to 6 Major A.W. GIBSON R.A.M.C. at 7.30pm. Mitchell Coff Ramy took over command of No 8 B.F.a from Capt Mitchell R.A.M. Cat 7.30 pm on return aroj leave.	Admissions O.R.B officers 3 wounded nil 9 Evacuated nil Sick nil 23 Evacuated nil 15

WAR DIARY
or
INTELLIGENCE SUMMARY.

Army Form C. 2118.

No 8. B.F.A.   May

(Erase heading not required.)

Hour, Date, Place.	Summary of Events and Information.	Remarks and references to Appendices.
R.16.C 24-5-15	7 A.M. Inspected the Ambulance. 11 A.M. Inspected the advanced dressing station with Capt Mitchell R.A.M.C. 12 noon The ADMS LAHORE Division visited the unit & inspected 3 cases of dental caries & 10 defective vision. 10:30 P.M. D.A.D.M.S. LAHORE Division visited unit & gave verbal instructions to send a motor ambulance to M.27.A.O.3 to take the C.R.A. General Johnson into Estair. He had met with a motor bicycle accident. Lt Warwick R.A.M.C. accompanied this ambulance. Orders issued to advanced dressing station re evacuation Cathures & Sick. (Appendix XX). and 5.	Admissions Evac. Duty Sick Died Remain wounded Officers nil nil nil nil nil O.R.B 1 1 1 nil 1 Sick. Officers. 1 1 nil nil nil O.R.B. 15 7 +2 nil 2.9. + to Letters Convalescent Coy.
R.16.C. 25-5-15.	9.30 A.M. DDMS Indian Corps visited the Ambulance. 11.45 A.M. ADMS LAHORE Division visited the unit. One of the motor ambulances attached to unit out of working order. Applied to have it sent for repair. Asst Surg Lamond transferred to H.L.S. for duty (Append 21) N.O. 10311 Pte J Kelly 1st Connaught Rangers died at 6 P.M. the result of shell wound of abdomen. Received orders to collect Sick & Wounded of Sirhind Brigade (Append 22)	Admissions Evac. Duty Died Remain wounded Officers nil nil nil nil nil O.R.B 11 1 1 nil 10 Sick. Officers, 1 1 nil nil nil O.R.B. 51 3.0 10x nil 40 + 8 to Convalescent Coy Sellers 2 to duty.

Army Form C. 2118.

WAR DIARY
or
INTELLIGENCE SUMMARY.   No S.B.F.A.

(Erase heading not required.)

May 1915

Instructions regarding War Diaries and Intelligence Summaries are contained in F.S. Regs., Part II, and the Staff Manual respectively. Title pages will be prepared in manuscript.

Hour, Date, Place.	Summary of Events and Information.	Remarks and references to Appendices
R.16.C. 26-5-15	9 A.M. D.D.M.S. Indian Corps visited unit. A.D.M.S. LAHORE Division inspected 2 cases of dental caries & one of syphilis anaemia. 5.30 P.M. DADMS LAHORE Division visited unit & gave instructions to send an ambulance to the Recruit Advanced Dressing Station at M.32.D map 1. 40,000 Bethune to collect the wounded from the H.L.I. Weather very warm & bright. Motor Ambulance 1113 Sent for repairs to Lillers. Motor ambulance no 1114 also requires to be repaired. There is now only one motor ambulance in working order.	Admission Evacuat. Discharge. Remain. wounded Officers nil nil nil nil O.R.B 11 14 3 5 Sick Officers 1 # nil nil O.R.B 8 12 8 nil 40
R.16.C. 27-5-15	In accordance with 31/58 of 26/5/15 the French interpreter CANCE transferred from unit. 9 A.M. DDMS Indian Corps visited the unit at 12 noon. ADMS LAHORE Division visited unit & inspected one case of dental caries & discharged him to duty. Weather cloudy & cool.	Admission Evac. Discharge. Remain. wounded Officers nil nil nil nil O.R.B 22 15 nil 12 Sick Officers nil nil nil nil O.R.B 9 6 # 21 22 19 M Gullar Remainder Company to duty

anf

Army Form C. 2118.

WAR DIARY
or
INTELLIGENCE SUMMARY.

No 6. B. F. A.

May 1915

(Erase heading not required.)

Instructions regarding War Diaries and Intelligence Summaries are contained in F. S. Regs., Part II, and the Staff Manual respectively. Title pages will be prepared in manuscript.

Hour, Date, Place.	Summary of Events and Information.	Remarks and references to Appendices
R.16.C. 26.5.15	9 A.M. DDMS Indian Corps visited unit. Paid Establishment at 2 p.m. Lt Noble RAMC handed over from unit to medical charge of 4th Suffolk Regt (Appendix XIII) Lt A.B.TOOTT (S.R.) R.A.M.C. reported for duty with this unit (Appendix XXIV). Received orders to collect wounded & sick from Jullundur B-gade. AWJ	Wounded / Officers / O.R.B. — nil / nil / nil / Rem. / nil 8 / nil 17 / nil nil / nil 3 Sick / Officers / O.R.B. — nil 18 / nil 9 / nil 10 / nil 21 * 1 to duty & 8 to convalescent company Lillers
R.16.C. 29.5.15	9 A.M. DDMS Indian Corps visited unit. Inspected dressing station at 12 noon. 12.30 p.m. ADMS LAHORE Divnon arrived unit & inspected 2 cases of dental caries. Lecture to Officers attached to unit at 3 p.m. Subject. The general organisation of the Army in the field (circular memo no.10 AWJ	Wounded / Officers / O.R.B. — nil / nil / nil / Rem / nil 5 / nil 5 / nil nil / nil 3 Sick / Officers / O.R.B. — nil 12 / nil 12 / nil 4 / nil 17 + 3 to duty, 1 to Lillers convalescent coy

Army Form C. 2118.

WAR DIARY
or
INTELLIGENCE SUMMARY.

No 8 B.F.A.
May 1915

(Erase heading not required.)

Instructions regarding War Diaries and Intelligence Summaries are contained in F. S. Regs., Part II, and the Staff Manual respectively. Title pages will be prepared in manuscript.

Hour, Date, Place.	Summary of Events and Information.	Remarks and references to Appendices
R.16.C. 30–5–15.	9 A.M. D.D.M.S. Indian Corps visited unit. 11 A.M. A.D.M.S. LAHORE Division visited unit. Sent one oxygen cylinder to advanced dressing station, two wheeled stretchers also sent for use at advanced dressing station. Received 145 respirators. Sent in indent for Smoke helmet. AwS.	Wounded: Officers nil, O.R.B nil. Sick: Officers nil, O.R.B 4. Killed: Officers nil, O.R.B nil. Missing: Officers nil, O.R.B nil. Remarks: nil 4 Sick: Officers 1, O.R.B 16. 11 6 1 16
12.16.C 31.5.15	9 A.M. DDMS Indian Corps visited unit. Received orders to collect of Ferozepore Bgde & 9 SIRHIND Brigade (Appx 25) ADMS visited unit at 1 p.m. & examined & carried 1 dental carriage & 2 cases of defective vision & one officer wounded orders to close (Appendix 26) Handed over dressing station to unit of F.F.Amb at 5 p.m. Received orders to close. also two wheeled stretchers carrier & one cylinder of oxygen. 3 Motor Ambulances sent to No 7 B.F.A for duty. 7 p.m. French Interpreter S. Le Moine reported for duty. [signature]	Wounded: Officers nil, O.R.B nil. Sick: Officers 1, O.R.B 4. Killed: Officers nil, O.R.B nil. Missing: Officers nil, O.R.B nil. nil 4 Sick: Officers 3, O.R.B 30. 30 +5 11 + 4 men to Convalescent Camp Sillers

Indus XXVI
21/31 May
55 p.m.

No 8. B.F.A

No 8 B.F.A. for duty aaa

Send two motor Ambulances to no 7 B.F.A. for duty aaa your bearer division to be withdrawn and advanced dressing station to be taken over tonight by no 7.B.F.A. aa your unit after evacuation todays first with aaa batth get wounded to no 7 B.F.A. LABORGUE till further instructions aaa. Hand over oxygen cylinder at dressing station to O.C. no 7 B.F.A. also two rebuild stretcher carriers.

Sd. J.M. Ryan
Lt Col
for A. Dms Hahoe

Appendix I.

21S D/1st May.   O.C. 8.B.7.a.

Your unit will march at 4 p.m. to BOESCHEPE via cross roads S of the R in RENINGHELST aaa. An officer to be sent in advance for billeting purposes, the billets to be selected near the baggage company of the train where you will remain closed waiting further orders aaa. No 112 P. will lead aaa. Report arrival time at POPERINGHE.

(Sd) B.B. Grayfoot
A.D.M.S. Lahore
Division

Appendix II
No 220 M/1st May.

O.C. No 8. B.F.A.

FEROZEPORE and JULLUNDER Bdes and 15 Lancers are marching tonight and sick should be collected from their units tomorrow morning aaa areas as follows. FEROZEPORE Bde. FONTAINE HOUCK and district N of METEREN aaa. JULLUNDR Bde THIEUSHOUK - COQ DE PAILLE (exclusive) N of FLETRE aaa. No 8 B.F.A. should hand over one motor ambulance to 112 I.F.A for collection of sick.

(Sd) B. B. Grayfoot
R.A.M.S.
ADMS. LAHORE DIV.

Appendix III.

222. D/2nd May. — O.C. 8. B.F.A
4.45 p.m.

Your unit will march tonight at 7.30 p.m. in rear of Divl. Amm. Column which is at BOESCHEPE. No. 8. B.F.A. to lead via BERTHEN, St. JANS, CAPPEL, BAILLUEL level crossing one mile south east of BAILLUL Stn. LE - PT. MORTIER aaa Orders for continuation of march will be issued by 1st Army aaa. No. 8. B.F.A will send three horse waggons to follow the Ferozepore Bde at 7.30 p.m. Route of Bde. METEREN NOOTE BOOM - DOEULIEU aaa. O.C. 112 B.F.A will send three horse waggons to follow the Jullundur Bde, route of Brigade FLETRE STRAZEELE VIEUX BERQUIN aaa All sick not evacuated from field Ambulances to be taken along with the Unit aaa Supply waggons will refil at FLETRE aaa. Divl. Head Qrs. will remain at POPERINGHE.

(Sd) J. M. Sloan
Lt Col
for A.D.M.S.
LAHORE DIV.

Appendix IV

24.8. of 6am May. O.C. 8. B.F.A.

Your unit will march tonight behind Sichime
Bde via Ll PETIT PACAUT L'EPINETTE - PT. LEVIS
LESTREM - PT RIQUEL to farm R16c and open
there in accommodation vacated by field Amb. Meerut
Division for reception of sick & wounded sea.
Bearers and Amb. waggons to be held in readiness
to move at short notice on arrival at new position.
Your unit will be evacuated at 6 p.m. tonight and
Report arrival immediately to this office.

(Sd) B.B. Grayfoot
Lt Colonel hmtb
A.D.M.S. Lahore Division

Appendix E

No 250 A/4th May.
9.6" a.m.

O.C. No 8. B.F.A.

To Officer British sick Hexippus Brigade aaa Bgde

Head Quarters Square M1 9

(Sd) J. M. Sloan
Lt Col
for ADMS Lahore Div.

Appendix VI Copy of order from ADMS Lahore Division D/8.5.15.

Please detail T.J. MITCHELL to proceed at once to No 8. B.F.A. to take over temporary command.

Sd. J. M. Sloan
Lt Col
for ADMS Lahore Div.

True Copy

D/8 6/15.

Sd. H.A. Hime
Lt Col RAMC
OC. No VII B.F.A.

Appendix VIII of S.4. msg. No 262.   O.C. No 8. B.F.A.
6.15.p.m.

A combined advanced Dressing Station will be formed tonight at
point M24.D.1. by No 8. B.F.A. and NB 112 I.F.A. aaa. The full bearer personnel
from each of these units will be dispatched to reach above point
by midnight aaa. They will bivouac for the night in the field
150 yards north of above point. Motor Ambulances to be parked
behind house at M24.D.1.1. aaa. Hopls. shelter trenches are on south
side of road at above point and files of these should be covered
as far as possible with straw aaa. Extra supply of bandages, dressings
and blankets should be sent with above Division aaa. No 112 I.F.A.
will send four motor Amb. waggons making up his number by Vauxhall
car from No 4.B.F.A. aaa. No 5.B.F.A. will send 6 motor Amb at
present with his unit aaa. Aid Posts of Jullundur Bde will be
closed at midnight as usual and Bearer divns to remain at Hurry
Stn till further orders aaa. Bearer divns Personnel of No 7.B.F.A. and
No 112.I.F.A. to move up in relieve to RUE DE PONCH at 6.a.m. 9.5.15;
to await orders aaa. British wounded to No 5. B.F.A. overflow to
No 7 B.F.A. Indian wounded to No 112 I.F.A. overflow to No 113.I.F.A. aaa.
Route to be strictly adhered to according to traffic map already
issued. Hyphen aaa.   Reports to A.D.M.S. at ESTAIRES.

(Sd) R.B. Grangott.
Col. gms
A.D.M.S. Lahore Div.

Appendix VIII   No 2 G 5-A/ 11th May.
10.30 am.

O.C. No 8. B. F.A

Dressing Station should be withdrawn forthwith aaa
Casualties to be collected nightly as usual by No 6 B.F.A
and No 112 I.F.A from Brigades aaa. Rendezvous road
junction M 27 D. at midnight aaa. British Bns 8. B. F. A.
Indian Bns 112 I. F. A.

(Sd) B.B. Grayfoot
Col. AMS
A.D.M.S. Lahore Division

Appendix IX   No 266 of 11th May
2.40 p.m.

O.C. No 6. B.F.A.

All NCR of Division ANS British and No
112 F.A. aaa. Election the arranged for behind Bde
tomorrow morning and till further orders in area
CROIX MARMUSE but for Yenzepre Bde aaa RIEZ
BAILLEUL aaa. Jullunden Bde and one battn. Yenzepre
Bde. remain in trenches aaa. Attention in drawn to my
No 38/2. dated 7th May aaa. Addressed No 6. B.F.A. and
No 112 F.A. copy AnSy B.F.A. and No 113 F.A.

Sd. J.M. Stopford
Lt/Col
for AAMG Lahore Division

Appendix X
291.B/15 May
4 p.m.

O.C. 8 B.F.A.

A combined advanced dressing Stn will be formed tonight at point N 24 D.1.1. by No 8 B.F.A & 112 F.A. aaa. The full bearer personnel of each of these units will march east of No 113 F.A & will be dispatched to reach above point by 9.30 p.m. aaa. Two motor Ambulances from each of these units to accompany Bearer Division forming with Ambulances will be held in readiness to move up when called for from advanced dressing Stn. until further orders wounded will be collected from Jullunder B de aaa. Beaux Divisional Personnel No 7 B.F.A. and No 113 F.A. to move up in turn to RUE DE PONCH by 9.30 p.m. aaa. One days ration to be carried by all aaa. British wounded to No 8 B.F.A. Indians to 112 F.A. overflow to No 7 B.F.A. and 113 F.A respectively aaa. Route to be strictly adhered to according to traffic map already issued by me aaa. Report BAPTING at ESTAIRES.

Sd. B.B. Grayfoot
Lieut. Col.
A.D.M.S LAHORE DIV.

Appendix XI.

To Unit Warwick Ramb.
S.B.Y.A

(1) The Bearer Division will parade at 8.30p.m tonight and march out to M27 D.1.1.

(2) You will be in command.

(3) Form a combined dressing station at M 27 D.1.1. with Bearer Division of No 112 F.Y.A

(4) Collect Sick & Wounded from JULLUNDUR BRDE. and evacuate to Tent Division.

(5) Two Motor Ambulance cars will accompany the Bearer Division – if more are required they will be sent up when you call for them.

(6) One days rations will be taken.

(7) Further orders will be sent to Advanced Dressing Stn M27D.1.

(8) Traffic route must be adhered to.

9 Refuse to Tent Division R.16.c.

4.25 p.m.
15.5.15.

(Sd). Y.J. Mitchell Captlamb
A.D.S. B.Y.A.

Appendix XII
248 D/16th May
9.10 p.m.

O.C. 8. B.F.A.

Collect sick of Sirhind Brigade at Med Quarters

X 4 B 8·3. Tomorrow 9.30 a.m.

Sd. B. B. Grayfoot
Major RMS
A D M S Lahore Division

Appendix XIII
No 291. 8/16th May

O. C. No 6. B. F. A.
R. 16. C.

Your Bearer Division should be withdrawn forthwith with the exception of one subdivision under an Asst. Surgeon and one motor Ambulance, which detachment should remain at Advanced Dressing Station and refuge for it should be carried out by you as required and. In addition casualties should be collected nightly at 9.30 p.m.

Sd. J. M. Sloan
Lt-Colonel
for Adm'g S. & how division

Appendix XIV.

To O.C. Bearer Division.

1. The Bearer Division less one Section (22 men & 5 stretchers, under an Assistant-Surgeon) will repair to Your Division above.

2. Sufficient dressings & equipment will be left behind with the Section.

3. One motor car will remain at the Dressing Station. The remainder to accompany the Bearer Division.

4. Casualties to be collected nightly at 9.30 p.m.

Sd. Y.G. Mitchell
Capt/Lamb
A.G. No S. F.A.

10.5-0.a.m.
18.5.15.

Appendix XV.
No 291. A/18 th may
6.45 p.m.

No 6. B.T.A.
R.16.l

No 6. B.T.A.
R.16.l

Move alones to Square R.15.D. after transferring wounded to no 4. B.T.A. aaa. unit to remain closed waiting further orders. aaa. After evacuation transfer all motor Ambulances to no 4. B.T.A.

Sd. B.B. Grayford.
Col. RMS.
ADMS. Tahoe Division

Appendix XVI.

No 294. A/ 15th May.
4.5 p.m

No 5. B. H. A.

Under instructions just received No 5. B. H. A.
is not to move a.a.a. Present arrangements hold good a.a.a
Cancel my 291.

Sd. B. P. Grayfoot.
Lt. Cmd.
A/No 5. Kohat Division

Appendix XVIII
296. At 18th May.
4.35 p.m.

No 8. B.Y.O. R.16.C.

Jullundur Brigade being retained tonight by Ferozepore Brigade aaa. Collect nearby Jullundur Brigade from tomorrow aaa. Brigade Head Quarters Square M.I.D.

A.Q.M.S
LAHORE DIVISION

Appendix XVIII

No 43/3
20.5.15

To
O.C. No 6. B.F.A.

Under orders of A.D.M.S. Indian Corps the barn with green doors at M.24.D.5.4. is to be formed as a permanent advanced dressing station. You are therefore detailed personally to arrange for the constituting of such by having the whole premises thoroughly cleaned out, latrines dug and cooking places and arrangements for both British and Indian troops prepared. Separate wards for British & Indian wounded to be made ready and a stock of clean straw stored on the premises ready for use when required.

All windows to the front should be covered so that lights used in the dressing station at night will not be seen from the front.

Carpentering fixings should be arranged so that if necessary there may be erected as extra cover sixty doors in the event of large numbers of wounded having to be handled.

A board with "Advanced Dressing Station Lahore Division" should be made & placed on the door of the building.

Sd. P.B. Grayfoot
Col. Ams.
A.D.M.S. Lahore Division

Appendix XIX

No 26.

Departmental order by Colonel B. B. Grayfoot R.M.S.
A.M.S. Natal Division.

Capt. T. J. Mitchell R.M.S. on being relieved of the command of No 8. B. F. a. by Major O. W. Gibson R.M.S. ordered from Hussrous Casualty Clearing Station, will report No 4. B. F. a. for duty.

Sd. B. B. Grayfoot
Col. R.M.S.
A.D.M.S. Natal

Appendix IX
49/4 of 24.4.15

Copy B no R.F.184 b/y dated 24.5.15 from the A.D.M.S
b Indian Corps.

Please give orders that no inhumation is to be done
at the dressing Station.

Patients are the soonest with green branches of trees
and sent with escort
Flights will be received at night on East, West
and South sides.

————

Forwarded for information & guidance

Sd. B.P Grayfort
Lt Col gmis,
A.D.M.S Lahore

Appendix XXI

367
Transfers

Extract from Field Ambulance orders by Major
A. W. Gibson R.amb. commdg. No 8. B. F. A.

25-5-15.

Asst Surgeon Lamond is directed to report
himself to the M.O. 1st H. L. Infy for duty.
A.D.M.S. no 31/06 dated 25th May

Sd A. W. Gibson
Major R.amb
O.C. No 8. B. F. A.

Appendix XXII
296 A/ 25th May.
11.25 a.m.

No 8. B. F. A.

Sick and wounded of Sialkot Bde. to be
collected tonight in addition to Ferozepore Bde. a.a.
Rendezvous as usual 9.30 p.m. a.a.o.

Sd. J. M. Sloan
Lieut.
for A. P. M. 8.

Appendix XXIII
31/64 of 28th May.

O.C. no 8 P.T.A.

Assist Lieut NOBLE R.A.M.C. to report
to O.C. 6th Suffolks for medical charge Regt. Square
R 20. A 5/6 relieving Capt J. D. WELLS RAMC

Sd J. M. Quin
Lt-Col. RAMC
for A.D.M.S.

App XIV

No. 29.

Regtl. order by Col. B. B. Grayfoot K.M.S. AQMG
Lahore Division of 28.5.15.

The undermentioned Ramb. Officers having
this day reported their arrival are posted for duty
as follows:—
Lieut. O. B. Foott (S.R.) Ramb. attd. to 6. B. F. A

Sd. G. M. Shan
Lieutenant
for Q. B. M. S.

Appendix XIV
2.16 AY 30th May
1.45 P.m

No 5. B.F.A

Collect with 4029pou Brigade tomorrow
Brigade will billet tonight RIEZ BAILLEUL
BOUT DEVILLE aue Bellue-alemish Sixteenth Brigade
L'EPINNETTE.

Sd. B.B Grayfoot.
Lt. jenl.
A.A.M.S. Leuiere

Gen W. J. O.

June 6/15

To D.A.G
3rd Echelon
Indian Section
Rouen

Herewith War Diary of
8. B. Fd. Ambulance for
June 1915.

A W Gibson
Major Rawl
OC 8. B. Fd. Amb
I.E.F

WAR DIARY
or
INTELLIGENCE SUMMARY.

(Erase heading not required.)

Army Form C. 2118.

Hour, Date, Place.	Summary of Events and Information.	Remarks and references to Appendices
1-6-15 R.16.C.	9 A.M. DDMS visited Ambulance. They have been closed since yesterday. At 12.15 p.m. the ADMS visited unit & inspected the Case of officer man who had been admitted the day before. Weather warm & bright. Board held on Capt H.J. Hore A.S.C. & Lt. Y.L. Lee 43 Brigade R.F.A. for fitness for regular Commission. AWF	<table><tr><td></td><td colspan="2">Adm</td><td colspan="2">Evac</td><td colspan="2">Died</td><td>Rem.</td></tr><tr><td>wounded</td><td>Officers</td><td>nil</td><td>nil</td><td>nil</td><td>nil</td><td>nil</td><td>nil</td></tr><tr><td></td><td>O.R.</td><td>nil</td><td>nil</td><td>nil</td><td>*3</td><td>nil</td><td>1</td></tr><tr><td>Sick</td><td>Officers</td><td>nil</td><td>nil</td><td>nil</td><td>nil</td><td>nil</td><td>nil</td></tr><tr><td></td><td>O.R.</td><td>nil</td><td>nil</td><td>nil</td><td>*7</td><td>nil</td><td>4</td></tr></table> * Sent Convalescent by letters.
2-6-15 R.16.C	Ambulance still closed. Cmdt Sergt Damond rejoined the unit. AWF	
3-6-15 R.16.C.	A.D.M.S. visited unit. Ambulance still closed AWF	Three cases of officers wounded were evacuated to ARQUES No.4 Stationary hospital.

Army Form C. 2118

WAR DIARY
or
INTELLIGENCE SUMMARY.
(Erase heading not required.)

Instructions regarding War Diaries and Intelligence Summaries are contained in F. S. Regs., Part II, and the Staff Manual respectively. Title pages will be prepared in manuscript.

Hour, Date, Place.	Summary of Events and Information.	Remarks and references to Appendices
R.16.C. 4-6-15	Pack Store Sergt Graham rejoined unit for duty. Lecture to Officers on general organization of the Army in the field.	One case (accidental wound of foot) still remaining out
R.16.C. 5-6-15	Ambulance still closed.	
R.16.C. 6-6-15	Nothing to note.	
R.16.C. 7-6-15	No. 255 Cpl Tophill R.A.M.C. and No. 3156 Cpl Davies Namt reported for pack store duty in place of No. 6520 Sgt Smallwood 2/Northern Frontier & No. 7761 Sgt Graham do.	
R.16.C. 8-6-15	Sgt Smallwood & Graham left unit to rejoin their own regiment. Four cases of mumps have occurred among the A.B.Corps.	

Army Form C. 2118

WAR DIARY
or
INTELLIGENCE SUMMARY.

(Erase heading not required.)

Instructions regarding War Diaries and Intelligence Summaries are contained in F. S. Regs., Part II, and the Staff Manual respectively. Title pages will be prepared in manuscript.

Hour, Date, Place.	Summary of Events and Information.	Remarks and references to Appendices
R.16.C. 9-6.15.	Unit Still closed. Hospt at Shri Rajin Hazdar transferred to Lahore C.C. Station.	
R.16.C. 10.6.15	2nd Class Asst Surg W.R. Kelly - Wickham reported for duty in place of 1st Class Asst Surg Johnson S.O. Rent auto nit: 7 B.F.A. sick. Lecture to officers on reorganization of medical services. July	
R.16.C. 11.6.15.	Nothing to report.	
R.16.C. 12.6.15.	Unit Still closed. A Case of suspected diphtheria occurred among the British personnel + was transferred to No. 7 C.C. Station at MERVILLE. Four Field Motor Ambulances attached to unit for duty.	

Gulab Singh & Sons, Calcutta—No. 22 Army C.—5-8-14—1,07,000.

Army Form C. 2118

WAR DIARY
or
INTELLIGENCE SUMMARY.
(Erase heading not required.)

Instructions regarding War Diaries and Intelligence Summaries are contained in F. S. Regs., Part II, and the Staff Manual respectively. Title pages will be prepared in manuscript.

Hour, Date, Place.	Summary of Events and Information.	Remarks and references to Appendices
R.16.C. 13.6.15.	Nothing Special to report.	
R.16.C. 14.6.15.	D.D.M.S. Indian Corps visited the unit at 12.30 p.m.	One case of accidental wound foot discharged to duty.
R.16.C. 15.6.15.	Lt. Warwick R.A.M.C. transferred to No. 7 B.F.A. as a temporary measure, motor ambulances sent to No. 112 I.F.A. for duty.	
R.16.C. 16.6.15.	The four motor ambulances rejoined this unit from No. 112 I.F.A.	
R.16.C. 17.6.15.	Nothing to report. Unit still closed.	
R.16.C. 18.6.15.	Nothing to report.	

Army Form C. 2118.

WAR DIARY
or
INTELLIGENCE SUMMARY.

(Erase heading not required.)

Instructions regarding War Diaries and Intelligence Summaries are contained in F. S. Regs., Part II, and the Staff Manual respectively. Title pages will be prepared in manuscript.

Hour, Date, Place.	Summary of Events and Information.	Remarks and references to Appendices
R.16.C. 19.6.15.	Nothing to report.	
R.16.C. 20.6.15.	Nothing to report.	
R.16.C. 21.6.15.	Capt BISSET R.A.M.C. left for England on short leave.	
R.16.C. 22.6.15.	Nothing to report.	
R.16.C. 23.6.15.	Medical board on Lt. G.W.BULKLEY A.S.C. for fitness for regular commission. Inoculation against enteric. 8 + 2 men of H.L.I. Carried out.	
R.16.C. 24.6.15.	Inoculated 51 men of 4th King's Liverpool Regt + 3 A.S.C. drivers of at 113 I.F.A. against enteric. 3 P.M. Lt. A.B. TOTTE R.A.M.C. temporarily transferred to medical charge of 1/Manchester Regt.	
R.16.C. 25.6.15.	Inoculated 7 men A.S.C. of R.113 I.F.A. + 3 A.S.C. of at 6 B.F.A. against enteric.	

Army Form C. 2118

WAR DIARY
or
INTELLIGENCE SUMMARY.
(Erase heading not required.)

Instructions regarding War Diaries and Intelligence Summaries are contained in F. S. Rgs., Part II, and the Staff Manual respectively. Title pages will be prepared in manuscript.

Hour, Date, Place.	Summary of Events and Information.	Remarks and references to Appendices
R.16.C. 25.6.15 (Continued)	12 noon Assist Surg CUMMINS of this F.Amb brought in by Lt JOHN. Showed act. Ill. J.F.Amb suffering from an over dose of morphia. It was understood that he made a statement to Lt JOHN that he took it with a view to taking his life. Report sent on to A.D.M.S. Lahore Division, & the patient admitted to No. 713 F.Amb for treatment. At about 7 p.m. on receipt of instructions from A.D.M.S. pending trial by Court martial CUMMINS placed under arrest under instructions from A.D.M.S. pending trial by Court martial. Cont'd	
R.16.C. 26.6.15	Nothing to report. Lecture to officers. Cont'd	
R.16.C. 27.6.15.	Nothing to report. Cont'd	
R.16.C. 28.6.15	Inoculation against enteric of 3 A.S.C. drivers attached to No. 113 F.Amb. Cont'd	

Army Form C. 2118

WAR DIARY
or
INTELLIGENCE SUMMARY.
(Erase heading not required.)

Instructions regarding War Diaries and Intelligence Summaries are contained in F. S. Regs., Part II, and the Staff Manual respectively. Title pages will be prepared in manuscript.

Hour, Date, Place.	Summary of Events and Information.	Remarks and references to Appendices
R.16.C. 29-6-15.	G.A.C. duties attached to Lt. 112 I.F. Ambulance inoculated against enteric. Capt. BISSET R.a.m.c. reported from short leave & proceeded in temporary duty D.D.M.S. at KESTREM.	
R.16.C. 30.6.15	22 men taken transferred train inoculated against enteric.	Aus. Gibson Maj. Lt. 23 S.B. I. Land

Serial No. 35.

12/6502

WAR DIARY
OF

No 8 British Field Ambulance. — Lahore Divn

FROM 1st July 1915 TO 31st July 1915

July '15.

Army Form C. 2118.

WAR DIARY
or
INTELLIGENCE SUMMARY.

(Erase heading not required.)

Instructions regarding War Diaries and Intelligence Summaries are contained in F. S. Regs., Part II, and the Staff Manual respectively. Title pages will be prepared in manuscript.

Hour, Date, Place.	Summary of Events and Information.	Remarks and references to Appendices
1st July 1915 B.16.C.	Ambulance still closed. Nothing to note.	
2nd July B.16.C.	36 men of Connaught Rangers inoculated against enteric fever. 2 men A.S.C. attached to 1-1 Gurkhas do. W/ 9076 Pte Clinton 1/Duke of Wellington's Regt left on short leave (7 days) for England. W/ 6576 Sgt Kendall J. 1/Duke of Wellington's Regt (Pack Store dept.) placed under arrest, on charge of drunkenness & obstructing the Military police. The Case of Memps A.V.C. admitted to 112 I.F. Amb. Coy	
3rd July B.16.C.	15 men A.S.C. w/ 1 coy L.D. Train & 2 men A.S.C. w/ 3 coy L.D.T. & 4 men A.S.C. w/ 2 coy L.D. Train & 7 men w/ 2 coy L.D. Train inoculated against enteric fever. Under instruction from A.D. Med. Lahore division Lt STRODE R.A.M.C. reported his departure yesterday, for probable charge of 14 Brigade Devonport Regt. relieving Lt HUTCHINSON R.A.M.C.	

Army Form C. 2118.

WAR DIARY
or
INTELLIGENCE SUMMARY.

(Erase heading not required.)

Instructions regarding War Diaries and Intelligence Summaries are contained in F.S. Regs., Part II, and the Staff Manual respectively. Title pages will be prepared in manuscript.

Hour, Date, Place.	Summary of Events and Information.	Remarks and references to Appendices
3rd July. R.16.C.	Took summary of evidence in case of Sgt Kendall & remanded him for F.G. Courtmartial. 3 Sunbeam motor Ambulances joined for duty in place of 3 Ford Cars withdrawn. Auj	
4th July. R.16.C.	13 men R.F.A. attached to head quarter Staff 16th Brigade innoculated against Enteric fever. One case of mumps A.B. Corps admitted to No 112 I.F Ambulance 8. P.M. Lt STRODE R.A.M.C. rejoined unit. Auj	
5th July. R.16.C.	7 men of Lahore Divnl Signal Coy innoculated against enteric. 12.30 noon Lt STRODE R.A.M.C. reported his departure on 7 days leave. Auj	
6th July. R.16.C.	Capt H.W.O. WALLER Lahore Divl. Artill. H.Qrs innoculated against enteric. Accts Serjt H.B.BLAKER rejoined from temporary duty with 1/1 H.L. Infantry. The under mentioned joined this unit from convalescent	

Army Form C. 2118.

WAR DIARY
or
INTELLIGENCE SUMMARY.

(Erase heading not required.)

Hour, Date, Place.	Summary of Events and Information.	Remarks and references to Appendices
6th July B.I.C.	Group dept MERVILLE for duty as grooms & batmen. No. 7522 Pte. McGREGOR, A. 1/H.L.I. " 18093 Pte. MULLIN, J. 4/Highland Transport Regt. " 14624 Gr. MELOY. R.F.A.	
7th July B.I.C.	Sgt. A. PRUDEN R.A.M.C. joined this unit from 3rd Brigade Field Ambulance 1st Division B.E. Force for duty as rack Store Keept. The undermentioned men left this morning to join 2/West Riding Regiment 13th Infantry Brigade I Division B.E.F. Rg. 8614 Pte WHITEAR. A. ⎫ " 8977 Pte DUDLEY. A. ⎬ 1st West Riding Regt. " 8985 Pte PAUL. A. ⎭	
8th July B.I.C.	L/C Carmarthal held on at 6676 Sgt. Kimbell J. 1/1st Bn of Wellington Regt. Found not guilty. Lt. A.B FOOT R.A.M.C. reported his departure for temporary duty with 4th London Regt.	

Army Form C. 2118.

WAR DIARY
or
INTELLIGENCE SUMMARY.

(Erase heading not required.)

Instructions regarding War Diaries and Intelligence Summaries are contained in F. S. Regs., Part II, and the Staff Manual respectively. Title pages will be prepared in manuscript.

Hour, Date, Place.	Summary of Events and Information.	Remarks and references to Appendices
6th July B.I.C.	Asst Surg. H.G. Greene reported his arrival for duty and assumed charge of this unit. 8 men of Lahore Divisional Signalling Coy & 5 Orderly No 2 & Coy A.S.C. were inoculated against enteric. A.D.M.S. Lahore Division visited the Ambulance. AnG	
9th July B.I.C.	Sgt. KENDALL left to rejoin his regiment. AnG	
10th July B.I.C.	Asst Surg CUMMINS rejoined this unit from hospital. Investigations were made by Capt BISSET Rome at CALONNE regarding the circumstances under which this Indian warrant officer is said to have taken an over dose of morphia. 26 men of Lahore Divisional Ammunition Column & 1 man of No 1 Coy A.S.C. inoculated against enteric fever. AnG	

Army Form C. 2118.

WAR DIARY
or
INTELLIGENCE SUMMARY.
(Erase heading not required.)

Instructions regarding War Diaries and Intelligence Summaries are contained in F. S. Regs., Part II, and the Staff Manual respectively. Title pages will be prepared in manuscript.

Hour, Date, Place.	Summary of Events and Information.	Remarks and references to Appendices
R.16.C. 11th July.	19 men taken bunewial at Ammunition Column, 1 man A.S.C. 41 Amst Surgeon, were innoculated against enteric fever. Amst Surgeon CUMMINS relieved from arrest, as supposed evidence was not forthcoming to justify his being put up for trial by court martial.	
R.16.C. 12th July.	Innoculation against enteric taken bunewial at Ammunition Column 25 men A.S. Corps 7 men 37 Lancers 1 Officer. Lt. A.S. TAYLOR R.A.M.C. joined the unit for duty. Lt. H.E. WARWICK R.A.M.C. rejoined from temporary duty from rely of B.F. Amb.	

Army Form C. 2118.

WAR DIARY
or
INTELLIGENCE SUMMARY.
(Erase heading not required.)

Instructions regarding War Diaries and Intelligence Summaries are contained in F. S. Regs., Part II, and the Staff Manual respectively. Title pages will be prepared in manuscript.

Hour, Date, Place.	Summary of Events and Information.	Remarks and references to Appendices
R.16.C. 13th July	Inoculation against enteric Labour Div: Ammun Column 37 men. Lt. T.W.R. STRODE Rawt rejoined from Short Leave Received orders from A.D.M.S. Labour Division to march to LA GORGUE on 15th July.	
R.16.C. 14th July	Inoculation against enteric Labour Div: Ammun Column 6 men. 7 men.	
15th July	Inoculated 1 officer 15th Lancers against enteric. Marched out from R.16.C. RUE DU PONCH at 12 noon & arrived at R. LA GORGUE at 1.15 p.m. & opened for reception of Sick & wounded in the Patronage P.T.O.	

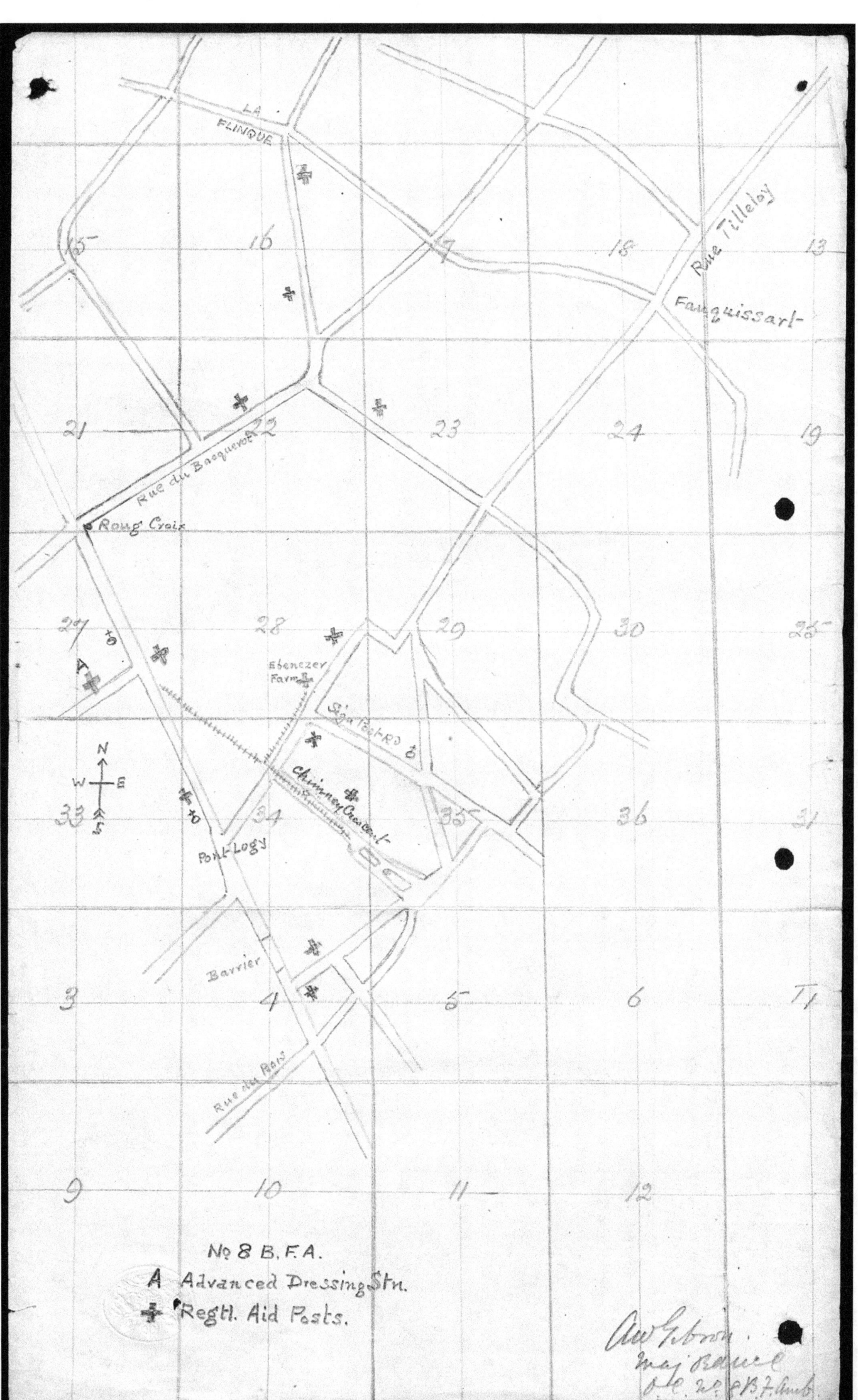

Army Form C. 2118.

WAR DIARY
or
INTELLIGENCE SUMMARY.
(Erase heading not required.)

Instructions regarding War Diaries and Intelligence Summaries are contained in F. S. Regs., Part II, and the Staff Manual respectively. Title pages will be prepared in manuscript.

Hour, Date, Place.	Summary of Events and Information.	Remarks and references to Appendices

		wounded	admitns	dischd	trans	dispd	Pavism
Officers	nil	nil	nil	nil	nil	nil
O.R.B	2	-	-	-	-	2
Sick						
Offrs.	nil	nil	nil	nil	nil	nil
O.R.B.	8	nil	-	-	-	8

15th July 1915.
The Patronage,
LA GORGUE.

Received orders from A.D.M.S. LAHORE Division to collect packet wounded from the right sub sector.

Took over the advanced dressing station at M.27.d from no. 112 I.F. Amb, & worked the various outposts to a-œstram their position. Maps showing aid posts & positions of dressing stations attached.

Sergt. Surg. H. R. GILLESPIE was sent out with bearer division to the Advanced dressing station.

The accommodation at the huts Chungin is sufficient for 200 patients. There are two buildings. One consists of two rooms. The ground floor is used as an operating room & surgery; at the first floor to accommodate 30 cases (sitting). The second building is a gymnasium with a large stage & can hold about 150 stretcher cases. Separate tent accommodation has been provided for infectious cases, & officers are sent to No. 7 B.F. Amb.

[signature]

Army Form C. 2118.

WAR DIARY
or
INTELLIGENCE SUMMARY.
(Erase heading not required.)

Hour, Date, Place.	Summary of Events and Information.	Remarks and references to Appendices
16th July 1915 St Patronage LA GORGUE.	ADMS Lahore Division visited Ambulance about 11 A.M. 13 Bn Lahore Divn Ammunition Column inoculated against enteric fever. No 2 Motor Ambulance Convoy evacuated the Ambulance at 10. A.M. & 5 P.M. [signed]	wounded adm. death died evac. remain. officers nil — — — — — O.R.B. 4 — — 2 4 Sick Offrs. nil — — — — — O.R.B. 8 — 1 — 8 8
17th July. Ste Patronage. La Gorgue.	A.D.M.S. Lahore Divn. visited the Ambulance at 11 A.M. Am't. Serj. CUMMINS committed suicide by shooting himself with his revolver. His body was discovered at 11.30 A.M. Court of enquiry held to enquire into the circumstances in which Am't. Serj. CUMMINS met his death. The finding of the Court was that this warrant officer had taken his life while temporarily insane. Three cases of mumps occurred among the A.B. Corps. They were sent to n°. 112 I.F. Ambulance [signed]			Admission	Discharge	Died	Evacuated	Remaining | Wounded Officers — — — — 1 — O.R.B. 2 — — 3 2 Sick Officers — — — — 1 — O.R.B. 13 — — 8 16

Instructions regarding War Diaries and Intelligence Summaries are contained in F. S. Regs., Part II, and the Staff Manual respectively. Title pages will be prepared in manuscript.

Army Form C. 2118.

WAR DIARY
or
INTELLIGENCE SUMMARY.
(Erase heading not required.)

Instructions regarding War Diaries and Intelligence Summaries are contained in F. S. Regs., Part II, and the Staff Manual respectively. Title pages will be prepared in manuscript.

Hour, Date, Place.	Summary of Events and Information.	Remarks and references to Appendices.
18th July. "The Patronage" La Gorgue.	11 a.m. A. Dms. LAHORE Division visited the Ambulance & inspected One Case of wound of hand. One Case of mumps received among the A.B. Corps. Ambulance cleared by a/c 2 M.A. Convoy at 11.30 & 5 p.m. Weather cold & cloudy. Amr S	**Wounded** Adm. Disch. Died Rem. Officers - - - - O.R.B. 2 - - 2 **Sick** Officers - - - - O.R.B. 13 - 7 22
19th July. "The Patronage" La Gorgue.	10.30 a.m. A. Dms. LAHORE Division visited the Ambulance & inspected three cases proposed for transfer to LILLERS as permanently unfit for duty. Two Cases of mumps received among the A.B. Corps. Ambulance cleared by a/c 2 M.A. Convoy at 11 a.m. & 6 p.m. Amr S	**Wounded** Adm. Disch. Died Rem. Officers - - - - O.R.B. 18 - 2 18 **Sick** Officers - - - - O.R.B. 13 1 - 13 21

Army Form C. 2118.

WAR DIARY
or
INTELLIGENCE SUMMARY.

(Erase heading not required.)

Instructions regarding War Diaries and Intelligence Summaries are contained in F. S. Regs., Part II, and the Staff Manual respectively. Title pages will be prepared in manuscript.

Hour, Date, Place.	Summary of Events and Information.	Remarks and references to Appendices.
20th July, "The Patronage" La Gorgue.	A.D.M.S. Lahore Division visited the Ambulance at 11 a.m. No. 7500 Pte BROWN 1/Seaforth Highlanders about died at 1.45 p.m. the result of shell wound of head. Weather bright & warm. One case of mumps received among the A.T. Corps.	**Wounded** Adm. Disch. Died Evac. Rem Officers — — — — — O.R.B 15 — 1 20 13 **Sick** Officers — — — — — O.R.B 16 — — 8 29
21st July "The Patronage" La Gorgue.	A.D.M.S. LAHORE Division visited unit at 11 a.m. & inspected S/S Blowers & Supports accidentally shot through the hand & 2 cases of Injection Teeth. 2 cases of mumps received among the A.T. Corps, & were transferred to No. 11.2 I.F. Amb. 12 men of A.B.C. (Bhutias) joined the unit for duty. No. 2 Bristol Convoy Cleared 2 sick & wounded at 11am [sig]	**Wounded** Adm. Disch. Died Evac. Rem Officers — — — — — O.R.B 25 — 5 — 33 **Sick** Officers — — — — — O.R.B 16 — — 8 37

Army Form C. 2118.

WAR DIARY
or
INTELLIGENCE SUMMARY.
(Erase heading not required.)

Instructions regarding War Diaries and Intelligence Summaries are contained in F. S. Regs., Part II, and the Staff Manual respectively. Title pages will be prepared in manuscript.

Hour, Date, Place.	Summary of Events and Information.	Remarks and references to Appendices.
22nd July. "The Patronage" La Gorgue.	No. 2 Indian Ambulance Convoy Cleared neck of wounded at 10.30 am. A.D.M.S. LAHORE Division inspected Central area at 11 A.M. Received orders from A.D.M.S. Lahore Division to form a decent advanced dressing station at LA FLINGUE (M.10.C) Sheet 36. Barves. Sent out an assistant surgeon with personnel & equipment to the above place. This dressing station to be a combined dressing station for British & Indian troops. No. 112 I.F.A also sent out a Sub. A. Surg with personnel & equipment to M.27. d. to form combined advanced dressing station with this unit. Weather Sunny & cool. [signed] D.D.M.S. Indian Corps inspected unit. [signed]	Wounded Adm. Disch. Died Evac. Remg. Officers – – – – – O.R.B 4 ⌀ – 16 19 Sick Officers – – – – – O.R.B 13 – – 15 35

Army Form C. 2118.

WAR DIARY
or
INTELLIGENCE SUMMARY.
(Erase heading not required.)

Instructions regarding War Diaries and Intelligence Summaries are contained in F. S. Regs., Part II, and the Staff Manual respectively. Title pages will be prepared in manuscript.

Hour, Date, Place.	Summary of Events and Information.	Remarks and references to Appendices.
23rd July "The Parsonage" La Gorgue.	Motor Amb. Convoy (No. 2) cleared the sick & wounded at 10.30 a.m. A.D.M.S. LAHORE Division visited the Ambulance & inspected all men with defective vision who was sent to No. 7 B.T.A. for transfer to ARQUES. Lt. FOOTT R.A.M.C. rejoined for duty. *[initials]*	**Wounded** Adm. Disch. Died Evac Rem Officers - - - - - O.R.B. 13 - - 6 26 SICK Officers - - - - - O.R.B. 37 3 - 16 59
24th July "The Parsonage" La Gorgue.	No. 2 Motor Amb. Convoy cleared the sick & wounded at 10 a.m. C.O.M.S. LAHORE Division inspected Ambulance at 11 a.m. & inspected 2 Cars of defective kits, 2 Eye cases & one of deformity right foot of Pte STEBBINGS 1/Manchester Regt. duty. Cases right foot & G.S. wound of chest.	**Wounded** Admit. Disch. Died Evac Rem Officers - - - - - O.R.B. 3 9 - 12 3 SICK Officers - - - - - O.R.B. 11 21 - 23 18
25th July "The Parsonage" La Gorgue.	Ambulance cleared by No. 2 Motor Amb. Convoy at 10.30 a.m. A.D.M.S. LAHORE Division visited unit at 11 a.m. & inspected 2 Cars of dental cases & one of defective vision. 2nd Lt. PATTERSON 1/Leicester brought in dead from G.S. shrapnel wound from Duvos & Prairie. dy.	**Wounded** Adm. Disch. Died Evac Rem Officers - - - 1 - O.R.B. 4 - 1 9 3 SICK Officers - - - - - O.R.B. 17 2 - 8 25

Army Form C. 2118.

WAR DIARY
or
INTELLIGENCE SUMMARY.

(Erase heading not required.)

Instructions regarding War Diaries and Intelligence Summaries are contained in F. S. Regs., Part II, and the Staff Manual respectively. Title pages will be prepared in manuscript.

Hour, Date, Place.	Summary of Events and Information.	Remarks and references to Appendices.
26th July 1915. "The Patronage" La Gorgue.	A.D.M.S. LAHORE Division visited ambulance at 10.30 A.M. No. 2 Motor Amb. Convoy cleared the sick & wounded at 11 A.M. 71 men of 1/Connaught Rangers innoculated against enteric fever. Also 1 man A.S.C. & 2 men R.A.M.C.	**WOUNDED** adm. / Disd Did / Evac / Remg Officers — / — / — / — O.R.B 17 / — / 4 / 18 SICK Officers — / — / — / — O.R.B 11 / 1 / 9 / 26
27th July. "The Patronage". La Gorgue.	Sick & wounded cleared at 10 A.M. & 6 P.M. by No. 2 Motor Amb Convoy. A.D.M.S. LAHORE Division visited ambulance. Inspected two cases of defective men & one case of accidental wound of hand caused by a bomb. 46 men 1/Connaught Rangers innoculated against enteric fever.	**Wounded** Officers — / — / — / — O.R.B 4 / — / 10 / 12 SICK Officers — / — / — / — O.R.B 20 / 4 / 8 / 39

WAR DIARY
or
INTELLIGENCE SUMMARY.
(Erase heading not required.)

Army Form C. 2118.

Hour, Date, Place.	Summary of Events and Information.	Remarks and references to Appendices.
28th July 1915 "The Parsonage" La Gorgue.	Ambulances cleared by a/c 2 M. Amb. Convoy at 10 a.m. A.D.M.S. LAHORE Division visited unit at 11 a.m., & inspected one man with defective vision & caries of teeth. Sgt TOPHILL R.A.M.C. rejoined from leave. Inoculated 16 men A.S.C. against enteric fever. [signed] Au.G.	**Wounded** Officers: Adm – , Disc – , Died – , Evac – , Rem – O.R.B: Adm 12, Disc 7, Died – , Evac 13, Rem 4 **SICK** Officers: – , – , – , – , – O.R.B: 14, – , – , 17, 31
29th " "	a/c 2 M.A. Convoy cleared sick & wounded at 10 a.m. D.D.M.S Indian Corps visited hospital at 11 a.m. A.D.M.S. LAHORE Division visited ambulance at 11.30 a.m. Inoculated one officer & 15 O.R. against enteric fever. Took in a French boy for treatment for wounds caused by a hand grenade. [signed] Au.G.	**Wounded** Officers: – , – , – , – , 1 O.R.B: 1, 1, – , 1, 3 **SICK** Officers: – , – , – , – , 1 O.R.B: 13, 4, – , 11, 29
30th " "	a/c 2 M.A. Convoy cleared the unit at 10.20 a.m. A.D.M.S. LAHORE Division visited this unit at 11.30 a.m. & inspected 2 men with defective teeth, 1 with defective vision & a case of wound Left hand. Asst Surg G.S. DINGAYAN reported for duty. 7 A.C. men inoculated against enteric fever.	**Wounded** Officers: – , – , – , – , – O.R.B: 5, 1, – , 4, 3 **SICK** Officers: – , – , – , – , – O.R.B: 12, 9, – , 10, 22

WAR DIARY
or
INTELLIGENCE SUMMARY.

(Erase heading not required.)

Army Form C. 2118.

Hour, Date, Place.	Summary of Events and Information.	Remarks and references to Appendices.
31st July 1915 "The Patronage" Le Gorgue	A.D.M.S. visited the unit at 10.30 A.M. O.C. 2 H.A. Cavalry Cleared off & inspected at 11 A.M. Inoculated 5 men of B.d.C. against enteric fever. Asst. Surg. E. Pell transferred for temporary duty with Connaught Rangers.	WOUNDED Adm. Disc Died Evac. Remg Officers - - - - - O.R.'s 4 2 - 2 3 SICK Officers - - - - - O.R.'s 20 8 - 7 27 A.W.Johns Maj. R.A.M.C O.C. No 8 B.F. Amb

Serial No 35.

121/6958

Aug '15

WAR DIARY
OF

No 6 British Field Ambulance

From 1st August 1915 To 31st August 1915

WAR DIARY
or
INTELLIGENCE SUMMARY.
(Erase heading not required.)

Army Form C. 2118.

Instructions regarding War Diaries and Intelligence Summaries are contained in F.S. Regs., Part II, and the Staff Manual respectively. Title pages will be prepared in manuscript.

Hour, Date, Place.	Summary of Events and Information.	Remarks and references to Appendices.
Patronage La Gorgue 1st August 1915	10. A.M. ADMS LAHORE Division visited unit. 11 A.M. Sick & wounded cleared by no. 2 M.A. Convoy. Received orders to march to VIEILLE CHAPELLE on 2nd & open for British pack of Meerut brigade & attached troops of 19th Division, & to transfer all patients remaining in the Ambulances to no. 7 B.F. Amb. Relieved orders to withdraw the heavier division section from the advanced dressing stations at No. 7 B.F & La Fringue. AwJ	Wounded: Officers – , O.R.B – , Comd was on ord pre sent – , Sick – , Ams 9 Officers – , O.R.B 22 9 1 39
Vieille Chapelle 2nd August	10.20 A.M. Sick & wounded cleared by no. 2 M.A. Convoy. Transferred remaining sick to no. 7 B.F. Ambulance. 2 P.M. Unit left La Gorgue having handed over billetting area & buildings used as hospital to no. 130 I.F. Amb. Meerut Division. 3.30 P.M. arrived at Vieille Chapelle & opened for reception of sick in the School buildings R.2 R.L.2.2. (Bethune sheet 40,000) AwJ	Sick: Officers – , O.R.B 6 7 – 6 Officers – , O.R.B 26 20 10 35

Army Form C. 2118

WAR DIARY
or
INTELLIGENCE SUMMARY.
(Erase heading not required.)

Instructions regarding War Diaries and Intelligence Summaries are contained in F. S. Regs., Part II, and the Staff Manual respectively. Title pages will be prepared in manuscript.

Hour, Date, Place.	Summary of Events and Information.	Remarks and references to Appendices.

Vieille Chapelle 3rd August	Received orders to collect sick from 81st Coy R.E. 19th Brigade at B.2.3.c. in addition to sick of Reserve Brigade.
	 11.30 a.m. 6 O.R's Labou Division wished unit at Warwick R.A.M.C. left proceeded to England on short leave.
	 13 men A.S.C. innoculated against enteric fever. AW
		Wounded
		 Officers O.R. Md sick Rems
		     x 38 3 — Nil
		         Sick
		 Officers
		 O.R. 1 32 3 — 1

4th August	11 a.m. Sick cleared by a/t. 2 M.A. Convoy Capt Foott R.A.M.C. returned from leave. 5 p.m. Sick cleared by a/t. 5 M.A. Convoy to Estaires. 3 A.S.C. men innoculated against enteric fever. AW	Sick O.R. B. Annlies — 72 Dis'd — 2 Rem'g — 6

Army Form C. 2118

WAR DIARY
or
INTELLIGENCE SUMMARY.
(Erase heading not required.)

Hour, Date, Place.	Summary of Events and Information.	Remarks and references to Appendices.
Vielle Chapelle 5th August	H.Q. the 5th Cav closed by 2/L M.A. Convoy. Included in Convoy held for return for pension on 2nd Lt R.C. Brown & Lt Lindlater of Manchester Regt & on Sgt Vidall by Battery H.Q. for pension for pensioner. Corp Sing who himself for temporary duty with machine gun section at MOLINGHAM. Capt Hay 13th # B.A.G.O admitted & transferred to No 7 London Base Hosp as a case of suspected typhoid. Received orders to send Lieut Neuve attached to IX Lancers duty with 1/1 H.L.I. Surrendered 3 Ad.br Drivers attached to IX Lancers against Battries. Any	Sick O.R.B. Admitted — 8 Evacd — 10 Remaining — 3
" 6 "	Capt Toste R.A.M.C. reported his departure for temporary duty with 1/1 H.L.I. 10.45 Am G.O.M.S. duties herewith evacked Ambulance & inspected the Caw & dispatch waggons. M Am. Ambulance closed by 2/L M.A. Convoy. Any	Sick O.R.B. Admitted — 5 Evacd — 3 Remg — 5

Army Form C. 2118

WAR DIARY

or

INTELLIGENCE SUMMARY.

(Erase heading not required.)

Instructions regarding War Diaries and Intelligence Summaries are contained in F. S. Regs., Part II, and the Staff Manual respectively. Title pages will be prepared in manuscript.

Hour, Date, Place.	Summary of Events and Information.	Remarks and references to Appendices.
Vieille Chapelle 7th August	11 am. Ambulance cleared by ad. 2 M.A. Convoy. The following men unevacuated against entente fever — 77 Battery 2 men. 81 Battery R.F.A. 3 men. 64 Batt. R.F.A. 2 men. A.S.C. 3 men totts 5 Ammn Column 2 men.	Sick O.R.B. Admitted — 5 Evacuated — 5 Discharged — 1 Remaining — 8
" " 8th "	A.D.M.S. Lahore Division visited Ambulance at 10.30 am & inspected 2 men with defective teeth. 11 am. Sick & wounded cleared by ad. 2 M.A. Conv. Medical transport field to Sgt. Maj. Morris & Sgt Maj Hayward, for jeparation for commission. 3 B.O.R. drivers attached to XV Lancers unevacuated against entente fever	Sick Officers — Admitted — 1 Evacd — 1 Remg — nil O.R.B. Admitted — 11 Evacuated — 5 Remg — 14

Army Form C. 2118

WAR DIARY
or
INTELLIGENCE SUMMARY.

(Erase heading not required.)

Instructions regarding War Diaries and Intelligence Summaries are contained in F.S. Regs., Part II, and the Staff Manual respectively. Title pages will be prepared in manuscript.

Hour, Date, Place.	Summary of Events and Information.	Remarks and references to Appendices.
Vieille Chapelle 9th August	11 a.m. No. 2 M.A. Convoy cleared Ambulance. Court of enquiry held to report enquire into the alleged absence of a/c 9.66, D/: Blackburrow. AuH	**SICK** Admd Evac? Disch? Died Remg Officers - - - - O.R.B 10 9 - - 15
" 10th "	10.30 a.m. A.D.M.S. visited Ambulance. 11.30 a.m. sick & wounded cleared by a/c 2 M.A. Convoy. Ca. 6 a.m. 13th H. battery admitted suffering from melancholia & transferred to a/c 7 London C.C. Station with a report on Case. Lt. Hubbard West Riding Regt rejoined from leave. Assist Surg Cannon resigned from temp duty with 1/Hawkshays. AuH	Officers - - - - O.R.B 16 8 3 - 18
" 11th "	Ambulance cleared by No: 2 M.A.C. at 11 a.m. AuH	Officers - - - - O.R.B 11 10 - - 19

Army Form C. 2118

WAR DIARY
or
INTELLIGENCE SUMMARY.
(Erase heading not required.)

Instructions regarding War Diaries and Intelligence Summaries are contained in F. S. Regs., Part II, and the Staff Manual respectively. Title pages will be prepared in manuscript.

Hour, Date, Place.	Summary of Events and Information.	Remarks and references to Appendices.

		Wounded			
		from	Evac. Sick	to dep	Rem
Officers		—	none	—	—
O.R.R					
			Sick		
Officers		1	1	—	—
O.R.R.		12	10	4	17

Vieille Chapelle
12th August

10.30 A.M. O.T.M.O. Labour Survey visited Ambulance & inspected 3 cases of telephone wires & three of defective truth.

11. A.M. Sick & wounded cleared by no. 2 M. A. Convoy.

Acting Sergt Kelly, Wound. emp. doing duty with this unit Admitted to hospital with tonsillitis & transferred to No. 7 London C.C. Station.

Cpl J. C. ——— against enteric fever.
Acting Sergt Blacker left on short leave for England.

P.S. Unwounded opened from leave

[signature]

Gulab Singh & Sons, Calcutta—No. 22 Army C.—5-9-14—1.07,000.

Army Form C. 2118

WAR DIARY
or
INTELLIGENCE SUMMARY.
(Erase heading not required.)

Instructions regarding War Diaries and Intelligence Summaries are contained in F. S. Regs., Part II, and the Staff Manual respectively. Title pages will be prepared in manuscript.

Hour, Date, Place.	Summary of Events and Information.	Remarks and references to Appendices.
Vieille Chapelle 13th August	Evacuated 3 cases of Influenza cases to No 4 Stationary hospital Argues per evacuation by No. Spec. about. 11 a.m. A.D. Med. insp. unit. 11.30 a.m. Ambulance cleared by No. 2 M.A.C. Received orders to collect wounded & form advanced dressing station at M.27.d. (Even Bars) troops in trenches Ferozepore Bgde & 1st battalion Jullunder Brigade. Medical board held on Lt. Kelly & King's Liverpool Regt. for permanent Commission. Asst Surg. Kelly, Northern Regimal unit, for duty. Ans I	**Wounded** Adm.ᵈ / Evacᵈ / Diedᵈ / Diedᵈ (wounds) Officers 1 / – / – / – O.R.B – none – **Sick** Officers 1 / 1 / – / – O.R.B 20 11 6 20
" 14th	10.20 a.m. A.D.M.S. Lahore division visited hospital to inspect inpts. Cases of 1/4th L.I. Also inspected 1 Case J.S. wound head. Ambulances cleared by No. 2 M.A.C. at 11.30 a.m. & 6 p.m. 3 Men O.S.C. inoculated against enteric fever. Ans I	Officers – – – – O.R.B 2 2 – 2 Officers 1 1 – – O.R.B 36 36 2 18

WAR DIARY
or
INTELLIGENCE SUMMARY.

Army Form C. 2118.

(Erase heading not required.)

Hour, Date, Place.	Summary of Events and Information.	Remarks and references to Appendices.				
			Wounded	Evac.	Sick	Rem'g
Vieille Chapelle	N. Am. C. Offr visited ambulance & inspected one case of defective vision.	Officers	—	—	—	—
15th August	11.20 sick & wounded cleared by No 2 M.A. Convoy to No 2 London C.C. Station	O.R.s	8	3	—	3
	19 A.S.C. men inoculated against enteric fever.			Sick		
	AwS	Officers	—	—	—	—
		O.R.s	29	13	4	30
" "	2 cases of defective vision evacuated to No 4 Stationary Hospital Aires for examination by eye specialist					
16th "	N. Am. C. Offr. labour division inspected ambulances & inspected 2 cases of defective teeth & one of gun shot wound. Left hand.	Officers	—	—	—	—
	Ambulances cleared by No 2 M.A. Convoy at 11 am & 5½ pm	O.R.s	8	1	2	9
	7 A.B.C. men joined for duty.					
	Lt. R.B. Wilson 129th Beluchis, admitted with Enteric fever and transferred to No 7 C.C. Station	Officers	2	1	—	1
	AwS	O.R.s	26	26	7	23

WAR DIARY
or
INTELLIGENCE SUMMARY.

(Erase heading not required.)

Army Form C. 2118.

Hour, Date, Place.	Summary of Events and Information.	Remarks and references to Appendices.
Vieille Chapelle 17th August	11 a.m. A.D.Med. Lahore Division visited Ambulance. 11.30 a.m. Ambulance cleared by nos 2 M.A. Convoy. No. 9421 Pte Hubbard rejoined from leave. 3 p.m. 5th Cavalry Column R.H.A. innoculated against enteric fever. AeB	Wounded — Officers: — Mis?: —, Acc?: —, Sick: 2, Pris?: —, Died: —, Rem?: 7 — ORs: —, —, 4, Sick, —, —, 7 Officers: 2, 3, 3, —, —, 23 O.R.s: 27, 22, 22, 5, —, 23
" 18th "	11 a.m. A.D.M.S. Lahore Division visited unit & inspected one case of defective teeth & one of defective vision. Sick & wounded cleared by nos 2 M.A. Convoy at 11.15 a.m. 5 p.m. AeB	Officers: —, —, 2, —, —, 5 O.R.s: 2, 4, —, —, — Officers: —, —, —, —, —, 22 O.R.s: 21, 15, 7, —, —, 22
" 19th "	11 a.m. A.D.M.S. Lahore Division visited Ambulance & inspected 5 cases of defective teeth. Sick & wounded cleared by nos 2 M.A. Convoy at 11.30 a.m. & 6 p.m. 2nd Lieut Kelly Woolson left for England on short leave. 7 men 4th London innoculated against enteric fever. AeB	Officers: —, —, —, —, —, 1 O.R.s: 1, —, —, —, —, 6 Officers: 1, —, —, —, —, 17 O.R.s: 26, 18, 15, —, —, 17

WAR DIARY
or
INTELLIGENCE SUMMARY.
(Erase heading not required.)

Army Form C. 2118.

Hour, Date, Place.	Summary of Events and Information.	Remarks and references to Appendices.

Remarks column details:

Wounded

	Adm?	W&?	D.ofW.	D.ofD.	Remg.
Officers	-	-	-	-	-
O.R.s	6	5	-	-	7

Sick

	Adm?	W&?	D.ofW.	D.ofD.	Remg.
Officers	-	1	-	-	-
O.R.s	31	14	2	-	32

(Wounded)

	Adm?	W&?	D.ofW.	D.ofD.	Remg.
Officers	1	1	-	-	1
O.R.s	10	9	2	-	6

Sick

	Adm?	W&?	D.ofW.	D.ofD.	Remg.
Officers	-	-	-	-	-
O.R.s	43	19	4	-	52

Vieille Chapelle
20th August

11 a.m. A.D.M.S. visited ambulance. Left 4 wounded cleared by adv. L.M.A. Convoy at 11.30 a.m. & 6 p.m.

Acting Surg. Blacker rejoined from leave.

16 men of 4th London sent inlisted against influenza.

AugJ.

21st

11 a.m. A.D.M.S. Lahore Division visited ambulance. 7 August.

1 case of infective eczema & two cases of wounds at hand.

No 2 M.A. Convoy arrived & 1st & sick evacuated at 11.30 a.m. & 2 p.m.

On orders acknowledged driving station to await arrival of A.D.M.S. 1st Army who inspected this division station at 4 p.m.

6 p.m.

Received orders to collect wounded from all points in the morning & inspect it at night.

Sgt Pritchard R.A.M.C. left for England on short leave.

12 men of Londons inoculated against influenza fever.

AugJ.

Army Form C. 2118.

WAR DIARY
or
INTELLIGENCE SUMMARY.
(Erase heading not required.)

Hour, Date, Place.	Summary of Events and Information.	Remarks and references to Appendices.
Vieille Chapelle 22nd August	10.30 A.M. A.D.M.S. Lahore Division visited Ambulance & inspected three cars of Motor Convoy. Six sepoy wounded cleared by No. 2 M.A. Convoy at 11 A.M. & 5 P.M. AMS	Wounded / Missing / Sick / D'd / Remy — Officers - 1 - - - / O.R.S 2 2 - - 6 / Sick — Officers - - - 1 - / O.R. 19 19 8 1 44
" " 23rd	Ambulance cleared by No. 2 M.A. Convoy at 10.45 A.M. & 6 P.M. 11.30 A.M. A.D.M.S. Lahore Division visited Ambulance and inspected 2 cars of Motor Convoy & one of departure convoy. Also 2 unfit men proposed to be sent down as 1st Cavalry 6/North Staffords admitted with penetrating 2nd Yorkshire wound of abdomen & transferred to No. 3 London C.C. Station Rouville AMS	Wounded — Officers - 1 1 - - / O.R.S 6 3 1 - 6 / Sick — Officers 2 2 - - - / O.R. 22 18 12 1 36
" " 24th	A.D.M.S. visited Ambulance at 11 A.M. Ambulances cleared at 11.30 A.M. & 5 P.M. by No. 2 M.A. Convoy. AMS	Wounded — Officers - 2 1 - - / O.R. 3 2 - 1 6 / Sick — Officers 2 1 - - 1 / O.R. 20 14 21 - 21

Gulab Singh & Sons, Calcutta.—No. 22 Army C.—5-8-14—1,07,000.

WAR DIARY or INTELLIGENCE SUMMARY.

Army Form C. 2118.

(Erase heading not required.)

Hour, Date, Place.	Summary of Events and Information.	Remarks and references to Appendices.
Neuve Chapelle 25th August	Sick & wounded cleared by №. 2 F.M.A. Convoy at 11 A.M & 6 P.M. on. No. 1 Lahore Division received ambulances at No. 3 F.M.A. Convoy 11.30 a.m.	**Wounded** 		Wnd	Evac	Disch	DieD	Remg	 	Officers	-	-	-	-	-	 	O.R.B.	5	6	1	-	4	 **Sick** 	Officers	-	1	-	-	-	 	O.R.B.	20	9	7	-	25
" " 26th "	Ambulances cleared by No. 2 F.M.A. Convoy at 11 A.M & 6 P.M 11.30 A.M. A Coy & №.3 Lahore Division received ambulance convoy	**Wounded** 	Officers	-	-	-	-	-	 	O.R.B.	4	1	-	-	7	 **Sick** 	Officers	-	-	-	-	-	 	O.R.B.	25	12	-	-	38
" " 27th "	11 am A & M.S. Lahore Division received Ambulance Ambulances cleared at 11.30 am by №.2 Ambulance Coy & at 5 p.m. by №. 8 F.M.A. Convoy. Lt. Hadden left to England on short leave. Received orders to hand over the Advanced Depot & station at M.2.7.d. to the present Division or 28th August & hand over present & equipment to the advanced dressing station at St. Vaast & from the Combined dressing station with No. III F.A. Amb.	**Wounded** 	Officers	-	-	-	-	-	 	O.R.B.	10	11	1	-	5	 **Sick** 	Officers	-	-	-	-	-	 	O.R.B.	17	12	16	-	27

Army Form C. 2118.

WAR DIARY
or
INTELLIGENCE SUMMARY.
(Erase heading not required.)

Instructions regarding War Diaries and Intelligence Summaries are contained in F. S. Regs., Part II, and the Staff Manual respectively. Title pages will be prepared in manuscript.

Hour, Date, Place.	Summary of Events and Information.	Remarks and references to Appendices.
Neuve Chapelle 28th August	11 A.M. A Bris Lahore Division wired for Ambulance Sickly wounded cleared by no 8 M.A. Convoy at 3 p.m. to no 7 C.C. Station Killers. Revmnt Surg. Sgt left for on ground on short leave. AWG	Wounded
		Officers — — — — — 1 Rem:
		O.R.B 4 3 — — 1 recovery
		S/ C K 6
		Officers — — — — 1 —
		O.R.B 13 13 3 — 3 24
29th "	A.D.M.S. Lahore Division wired Ambulance at 11.30 AM & accepted transferred the personnel & equipment of bearer division from advanced dressing station M.27.d to St Vaast handing over the former dressing station to Meerut Division. Confined during station formed at St Vaast in conjunction with no 111 J.F.Amb. Received instructions to hand detail a.b.b f. duty for 24 hours at advanced dressing station. The arrangement to be carried on for a few alternate days by this unit & at 111 J.F.Amb. Sgt Turpin R.A.M.C reported from short leave AWG Constr. cleared at 4 p.m. by 22 S M.O Convoy.	Wounded
		Officers — — — — 1 3
		O.R.B 2 5" — — 1
		S/ C K
		Officers 1 1 — — — —
		O.R.B 12 8 4 — 1 26
30th "	12 Noon A Bris Lahore Division wired for ambulance & inspected one B.x. Case. Received orders to hand over command of unit to Maj. H.W. Russell R.A.M.C on 31-8-15 & proceed to Kettes to command no 9 C.C. Station. Command handed over by no 8 M.A. Convoy at 4 p.m. AWG	Wounded
		Officers — — — — 1 3
		O.R.B 2 — 1 1 2
		S/ C K
		Officers 2 — — — 2
		O.R.B 22 6 6 — — 36

WAR DIARY or **INTELLIGENCE SUMMARY**

Army Form C. 2118.

No. 8 B.G.A.

(Erase heading not required.)

Hour, Date, Place.	Summary of Events and Information.	Remarks and references to Appendices.
Neuve Chapelle. 31–8–15	12 noon A.D.M.S. visited Ambulance. 3 p.m. Handed over Command of Ambulance to Maj. H.W. Russell R.A.M.C. Took over Command of Ambulance from Maj. A.W. John Reeve. Churchson May Reeve Maxwell Rays Reeve	Wounded: Adm evac Disch Rem Officers — — — — O.R.B 3 — — 5 Sick Officers 1 — — 1 O.R. 13 16 14 7 31
1–9–15	A.D.M.S. visited hospital 12.15 p.m. Orders received to take over GREEN BARN (to clear TELLUNDAR BGDE) and transfer personnel there housed at our hospital to 10 p.m. Wounded at 4 p.m. Lieut WARWICK RAMC superseded this exchange. A Surgeon BLAKER put in charge. ADVANCED DRESSING STN (GREEN BARN) in place of A Surg. DINGAVAN RAMC. relieved for duty here. DADMS came late in the afternoon. I took round all the ADS posts in the afternoon with Lieut WARWICK + Capt FOOT 24 Stretcher Bearers sent to G. BARN – 16 ft hurdles + 8 m.	
2–9–15		

Sept. 1915
121/7286
Serial No. 35.

Confidential

121/7286

War Diary

of

No 8 British Field Ambulance.

FROM 1st September 1915. TO 30th September 1915.

Army Form C. 2118.

WAR DIARY
or
INTELLIGENCE SUMMARY.
(Erase heading not required.)

Instructions regarding War Diaries and Intelligence Summaries are contained in F. S. Regs., Part II, and the Staff Manual respectively. Title pages will be prepared in manuscript.

Hour, Date, Place.	Summary of Events and Information.	Remarks and references to Appendices.
Vieille Chapelle		
1-9-15	ADMS visited hospital 12.15 p.m. Orders received to take over GREEN BARN (G. chan TELLONDAR BOE) and transfer personnel there known at a time mentioned later (10 a.m.). Evacuated at 4 p.m.	Wounded: Officers — Admitted -, Evacuated -, Discharged -, Died -, Remg -; O.R.B -, 3, -, -, 4. Sick: Officers 1, 1, -, -, 1; O.R.B 10, 7, 3, -, 29. Transport engine
2-9-15	LIEUT WARWICK inspected the above charge. A Surgeon BLAKER (not in charge of the Advanced dressing station (GREEN BARN) in place of Senior surg. DINGAVAN who returned here for duty. D.A.D.M.S. came late in the afternoon. I visited all No out posts. In the afternoon with Lieut WARWICK Lieut. FOOTT 2nd Scottish Horse was sent to G. BARN 16 for link & in advent.	Wounded: Officers -, 2, 1, -, 1; O.R.B -, 2, 1, -, 1. Sick: Officers 1, 2, -, -, 2; O.R.B 29, 12, 10, -, 36.
3-9-15	A.T.M.S. visited Post No 30 one 8 BFA Ban one S.VAAST (NAAST) as well as GREEN BARN. R. MO. to live at S.VAAST. The personnel of S.VAAST is furnished by 111 I.F.A. an officer of 8 BFA & attend S.VAAST a alternate days with an officer of 111 I.F.A.	Wounded: Officers -, -, -, -, -; O.R.B 2, -, -, -, 3. Sick: Officers 1, -, -, -, 1; O.R.B 16, 19, 13, -, 20.

WAR DIARY or INTELLIGENCE SUMMARY.

Army Form C. 2118.

(Erase heading not required.)

Hour, Date, Place.	Summary of Events and Information.	Remarks and references to Appendices.
Villa au Bois 4-9-15.	A.D.M.S. visited the Ambulance at 10.30 A.M.	Wounded — Admitted / Evacuated / Discharged / Died / Remaining Officers: - / - / - / - / - O.R.B: 2 / 1 / 1 / - / 2 Sick Officers: 2 / 1 / - / - / 2 O.R.B: 10 / 11 / 5 / - / 14
5-9-15	A.D.M.S. visited the Ambulance at 10.30 A.M.	Wounded Officers: - / - / - / - / - O.R.B: 1 / - / 1 / - / 2 Sick Officers: 3 / - / 1 / - / 2 O.R.B: 21 / 11 / 1 / - / 23
6-9-15	A.D.M.S. visited the Ambulance at 10.30 A.M. Sanitary Officer future visited the Ambulance at 10.15 A.M.	Wounded Officers: - / - / - / - / - O.R.B: 3 / 2 / 1 / - / 3 Sick Officers: - / - / - / - / - O.R.B: 25 / 16 / 5 / - / 27
7-9-15	Lt Col Beevers went up to the Advanced Dressing Station (ST. VAAST) where Lt WARWICK is upon the wound. A.D.M.S. visited Ambulance 10.30 A.M. I visited the trenches and took in the afternoon and inspected the road repairs.	Wounded Officers: - / - / - / - / - O.R.B: 3 / 2 / - / - / 4 Sick Officers: - / - / - / - / - O.R.B: 29 / 15 / 1 / - / 33

WAR DIARY
or
INTELLIGENCE SUMMARY.
(Erase heading not required.)

Army Form C. 2118.

Hour, Date, Place.	Summary of Events and Information.	Remarks and references to Appendices.
Vieille Chapelle 8-9-15.	ADMS visited Ambulance 10.30 A.m. 20 Bearers sent up to repair S.VAAST Road. An officer apparently S/Lt visited transport lines & asked questions about walls cook & bottom etc. Sgt. BROWNING replied the matter to me. I wrote particulars & reported to ADMS	**Wounded** Officers — — — — Admitted/Evacuated/Discharge/Died/Remaining O.R.B 2 4 1 — 1 **Sick** Officers 1 — — — — O.R.B 17 10 12 — 28
9-9-15	Nothing to record.	**Wounded** Officers — — — — — O.R.B 1 1 — — 1 **Sick** Officers — — — — — O.R.B 13 13 8 — 20
10-9-15	ADMS visited Ambulance 10.30. Aut Surg. LAMOND replaced at GREEN BARN by Aut Surg. FOX.	**Wounded** Officers — — — — — O.R.B 3 2 — — 2 **Sick** Officers — — — — — O.R.B 15 4 4 1 30
11-9-15	ADMS & DDMS visited Ambulance at 10.30 AM.	**Wounded** Officers — — — — — O.R.B 8 1 1 — 8 **Sick** Officers — — — — — O.R.B 12 13 1 — 26

Army Form C. 2118.

WAR DIARY
or
INTELLIGENCE SUMMARY.
(Erase heading not required.)

Hour, Date, Place.	Summary of Events and Information.	Remarks and references to Appendices.
Vieille Chapelle 12 - 9 - 15	ADMS visited Hospital 10.30 am	Wounded Admitted Evacuated Discharged Died Remaining Officers — 2 — — — 2 O.R.B. — 8 — — — 2 Sick Officers 1 3 1 — — 2 O.R.B. 15 12 3 — — 28
13 - 9 - 15	ADMS & DADMS visited hospital 10.30 am. Inspected three hospital by OC 16g Lahore Divisional Train. 3 pm.	Wounded Officers 4 4 — — — 2 O.R.B. — — — — — — Sick Officers — — — — — — O.R.B. 10 6 6 — — 26
14 - 9 - 15	So O'Connaught Rangers inoculated against Typhoid. Commenced construction of Reception Shed in the yard of hospital (School V. Chapelle). Ast S. Surgeon relieved Ast S. I.H. at Green Barn. Cann oil supplied in bulk to Green Barn and aid posts.	Wounded Officers — 2 — — — — O.R.B. — — — — — 4 Sick Officers — — — — — — O.R.B. 17 16 2 — — 25
15 - 9 - 15	ADMS & DADMS visited hospital 10.30 am. With 2.0 Bearer near Svarat — in afternoon 3rd Ma Kaylors hit by piece of bursting shell, 3 sent to hospital IIIrd F.A. (Calc 2 of these wounded in regiment)	Wounded Officers — — — — — — O.R.B. 1 3 — — — 2 Sick Officers — — — — — — O.R.B. 19 10 4 — — 30

WAR DIARY
or
INTELLIGENCE SUMMARY.

(Erase heading not required.)

Army Form C. 2118.

Hour, Date, Place.	Summary of Events and Information.	Remarks and references to Appendices.
Neuve Chapelle. 16-9-15	A Bn is visited Hospital 10.30 am	Wounded / Admitted / Evacuated / Disposal / Died / Remaining Officers - - - 1 - 1 O.R.B - 4 3 - - 2 Sick Officers 1 - - - - 1 O.R.B 19 32 5 - - 22
17-9-15	Visited 5 and Green Barn Plumetta & investigate the water supply of Green Barn. Asst S. Blake relieves Asst S. Dungan at GREEN BARN. Do Bennen relieved by Do Mess.	Wounded Officers - - - - - - O.R.B - 1 - - - 2 Sick Officers 1 - - - - 1 O.R.B 8 9 2 - - 19
18-9-15	A Bn is visited hospital 10.30 am. Lt. Warwick proceeds on 2 mths leave commencing 19.9.15. he is relieved by Lieut MAPOTHER from 7 BFA.	Wounded Officers - - 3 - - 7 O.R.B - - - - - - Sick Officers 1 - - 1 - 1 O.R.B 18 3 5 - - 29
19-9-15	A Bn is visited hospital 10.30 am. Shed in hospital yard in completion.	Wounded Officers - - - - - - O.R.B - 4 2 - - 2 Sick Officers 1 1 1 - - 2 O.R.B 24 19 4 - - 30

Army Form C. 2118.

WAR DIARY
or
INTELLIGENCE SUMMARY.

(Erase heading not required.)

Hour, Date, Place.	Summary of Events and Information.	Remarks and references to Appendices.
Vielle Chapelle 20-9-15	ADMS visited SP at 10.30. DDMS " " in afternoon	Wounded / Admitted / Evacuated / Died / Remg. Officers — — — — — O.R.s 1 — — — 3 Sick Officers 2 2 — — 3 O.R.s 10 11 3 — 26
21-9-15	20 Bearers at dressing station Green BARN relieved by 20 others	Wounded Officers 1 1 — — 3 O.R.s — — — — — Sick Officers 3 3 — — 1 O.R.s 16 10 6 — 26
22-9-15	ADMS & DDMS came in the morning. Asst Surgeon LATONA relieved Asst Surg GINGEVAN at GREEN BARN. Took over relieved BREWERY a/c as hospital for sitting cases in case of necessity	Wounded Officers — — — — — O.R.s 4 3 — — 4 Sick Officers 2 2 — — — O.R.s 13 7 11 — 21
23-9-15	ADMS visited hospital at 11 am. 'C' Section opened up at BREWERY	Wounded Officers — — — — — O.R.s 7 1 — — 10 Sick Officers 1 — — — 1 O.R.s 9 6 13 — 11

WAR DIARY
or
INTELLIGENCE SUMMARY.
(Erase heading not required.)

Army Form C. 2118.

Hour, Date, Place.	Summary of Events and Information.	Remarks and references to Appendices.
VIELLE CHAPELLE 24 - 9 - 15	MOs. 2, Captⁿ ALLEN + GARSON - Asst Surg. 4, CREAIS, ELLOY, D'ABREU & SWEENEY. Ward Orderlies 4, + 100 BEARERS. Tethers with One HORSE AMBULANCE + four MOTOR AMBULANCES + late One native cook were sent to this Ambulance from No 7 AFA. One HORSE AMBULANCE from 112 IFA. Came here for duty. 4 Sweepers / 2 Bn Sanitary Section Came here for duty. 1 Orderly / The ADVANCED DRESSING STATION (GREEN BARN) was occupied ready for any emergency at 7.30 pm. Personnel - Capt FOOTT (in command) Capt ALLAN. Asst Surgeons D'ABREU, LAMOND, SWEENEY. Nursing Orderlies 2 Orderly from San. Sect 1, Batmen 1, ABC 80 (No7 + No 8). Wardservant 2 Cooks 1, Bheestie 1, Sweepers 3 (2 from San Sect). Two motor ambulances were drawn up at M26.C.8.8 (near Cross Barrier) for taking cases, who would be marched in batches of 4 up from the Dressing Station by a tent K in his opt. In case of a rush of wounded, The cyclist would bring a message (time stated) with the number of ambulances required. Ambulances would then be despatched. Ambulances intended from V.Chapelle till the demand had been supplied. This K arrangement was introduction and an improvising	Wounded 		Admitted	Evacuated	Discharged	Died	Remaining
---	---	---	---	---	---
Officers	1	-	-	-	1
O.R.B	2	8	2	1	2 | Sick |	Admitted	Evacuated	Discharged	Died	Remaining
---	---	---	---	---	---
Officers	1	1	-	-	¾
O.R.B	13	10	3	1	11	

Army Form C. 2118.

WAR DIARY
or
INTELLIGENCE SUMMARY.

(Erase heading not required.)

Hour, Date, Place.	Summary of Events and Information.	Remarks and references to Appendices.

VIEILLE CHAPELLE
24-9-15
(Contn.)

accumulation of Ambulances in a dangerous spot.

BREWERY VIEILLE CHAPELLE. was opened for sitting cases only. The staff was as under. M.O. CAPT BISSET (in charge) Lt STRODE. Asst. Surgeons FIN, FIDO, ELLDY. Part of the Sergeants PRUDEN, TOPHILL. Nursing orderlies 5, and Store Keeper 1. 'C' section was opened here together with its personnel.

SCHOOL VIEILLE CHAPELLE. - was opened for lying cases. M.O. CAPT GARSON, LIEUT MAC POTHER - Assist Surg GREENE, GILLESPIE DINGAYAN, BLAKER, CREAIS. Pack store i/c GRADY, DAVIES Nursing orderlies 5, + other personnel.

Sick cases were detained till 14 in a sufficient number to fill an Ambulance. They were accumulated. They were then sent by line Ambulance to No 4 an advance No to No 7.

All cases in the hospital were evacuated in ambulances.

3 sets of orders were issued - Given Barn - hospital orders + operation orders.

Army Form C. 2118.

WAR DIARY
or
INTELLIGENCE SUMMARY.

(Erase heading not required.)

Instructions regarding War Diaries and Intelligence Summaries are contained in F. S. Regs., Part II, and the Staff Manual respectively. Title pages will be prepared in manuscript.

Hour, Date, Place.	Summary of Events and Information.	Remarks and references to Appendices.
VIEILLE CHAPELLE. 25-9-15	Nothing occurred during night 24/25. Very few cases $ (wounded) came to during the day - several yers cases came in. Lieut Napier. 47 Sikhs was admitted in a dying state and died soon after admission. Visited GREEN BARN during the afternoon. Found everything in working order. Motor Ambulances were recalled at 10 pm to return at 7 am 26/9/15	Wounded Adm? Evac? Sick? Died Remy Officers — 1 — — — O.R.B 9 5 — — 6 Sick Officers " — — — — O.R.B 26 34 3 — —
26-9-15.	DDMS visited the School at 10.30 am. 6 B.S. wagons went to Bearer Sec to [Casualty] CROIX BARBÉE to relieve 80 Bearers at GREEN BARN at 5.45 AM. 2 Horse Ambulances sent to CROIX BARBÉE at 6 am. Very few wounded admitted during the day.	Wounded Officers 76 5 — 2 — O.R.B 61 66 — — — Sick Officers — nil — O.R.B

WAR DIARY
or
INTELLIGENCE SUMMARY.
(Erase heading not required.)

Army Form C. 2118.

Hour, Date, Place.	Summary of Events and Information.	Remarks and references to Appendices.
VIELLE CHAPELLE 27-9-15	80 bearers at GREEN BARN relieved by 50 sent up in Gp. Wagons. Horse Ambulance withdrawn at 5pm, none to be replaced unless ordered. Asst Surg LYONS returned by Portsburg F.A.D. 5 Large Motor Ambulances by MOTS were sent under command of Capt BILLET to LILLERS to aid in evacuating C.C.S. No 6 - One Car left here at 8.45 pm.	Wounded — Admitted / Evacuated / Discharge and / Remaining Officers 2 / 1 / — / — O.R.s 5 / 3 / — / —
28-9-15	Ambulances returned from LILLERS at 9 a.m. Under orders from ADMS all returned personnel and cars to join their units. Lieut HAPOTHER returned to No.7. B.F.A.	Wounded Officers 1 / 1 / — / — O.R.s 3 / 2 / — / 1 Sick Officers 6 / 1 / — / — O.R.s 6 / 3 / — / 3
29-9-15	By orders of ADMS one Motor Ambulance sent to ESSARS to a newly formed motor field Ambulance 113. Only one Car is now kept at GREEN BARN. The BREWERY is closed down. The equipment of "C" section is checked. The equipment of "D" section is also checked.	Wounded Officers — / — / — / — O.R.s 4 / — / — / 3 Sick Officers — / — / — / — O.R.s 1 / 3 / — / —

Army Form C. 2118.

WAR DIARY
or
INTELLIGENCE SUMMARY.

(Erase heading not required.)

Instructions regarding War Diaries and Intelligence Summaries are contained in F. S. Regs., Part II. and the Staff Manual respectively. Title pages will be prepared in manuscript.

Hour, Date, Place.	Summary of Events and Information.	Remarks and references to Appendices.
VIEILLE CHAPELLE 30-9-15	A.D.M.S. came to R. at 10.30 a.m. Hospital open as usual for sick & wounded. GREEN BARN & ADVCT. DRESSING ST. remained working as usual for today - No 111 F.A. on duty today. 8 B.F.A. known. J.M. Russell Major R.A.M.C. O.C. No 6 B.F.A.	Wounded / Sick Admitted / Died / Evac. / Died Officers — — — — OR's — — — 3 Sick Officers — — — — OR's 7 — — 7

121/7601

Serial No. 35

Confidential

War Diary

of

No 8 British Field Ambulance

FROM 1st October 1915 TO 31st October 1915

Army Form C. 2118

9 NOV 1915

WAR DIARY
or
INTELLIGENCE SUMMARY.
(Erase heading not required.)

Instructions regarding War Diaries and Intelligence Summaries are contained in F. S. Regs., Part II, and the Staff Manual respectively. Title pages will be prepared in manuscript.

Hour, Date, Place.	Summary of Events and Information.	Remarks and references to Appendices.
VIELLE CHAPELLE		
1 – 10 – 15	ADMS visited SP at 10.30. Lt STRODE is on duty at ST VAAST. Bearers at GREEN BARN changed. Asst Surg FOX relieves Asst Surg DUNDAVAN at the GREEN BARN.	
2 – 10 – 15	ADMS visited hospital at 10.30. A case of suspected CHOLERA was admitted to hospital - stools examined bacteriologically – NEGATIVE	
3 – 10 – 15	Commence collecting sick from the S.R.IND BGDE. Inspect GREEN BARN & ST VAAST.	
4 – 10 – 15	ADMS visited hospital at 11.30. Lt WARWICK returns from leave. A man 61239 T/JR ST ELDRIDGE A.S.C. was brought in dead – 2 p.m. in haste. Patient was sent to Canadian Mob. Lab. Henries. the examination proved not there was no trace of attalonent poison.	

Army Form C. 2118.

WAR DIARY
or
INTELLIGENCE SUMMARY.

(Erase heading not required.)

Instructions regarding War Diaries and Intelligence Summaries are contained in F. S. Regs., Part II, and the Staff Manual respectively. Title pages will be prepared in manuscript.

Hour, Date, Place.	Summary of Events and Information.	Remarks and references to Appendices.
VIELLE CHAPELLE		
5 - 10 - 15.	Asst Surg COOMBES went to ADV DRESSG STATION.	
6 - 10 - 15.	Asst Surg FOX returned from ADV. DRESSG. STATN. ADMS visited hospital 10.30 a.m.	
7 - 10 - 15.	A.D.M.S. visited hospital. D.D.M.S. & Col. KIRKPATRICK visited hospital in morning.	
8 - 10 - 15.	Nothing to note.	

Army Form C. 2118.

WAR DIARY
or
INTELLIGENCE SUMMARY.
(Erase heading not required.)

Instructions regarding War Diaries and Intelligence Summaries are contained in F. S. Regs., Part II, and the Staff Manual respectively. Title pages will be prepared in manuscript.

Hour, Date, Place.	Summary of Events and Information.	Remarks and references to Appendices.
VIEILLE CHAPELLE 9-10-15	ADMS visited hospital at 10.30 am. Revd ROYLE from CAVALRY FIELD AMBULANCE (AMBALA) reported his arrival to be attached to his FIELD AMBULANCE.	
10-10-15	ADMS & DADMS visited hospital 10.30 am.	
11-10-15	Assist Surg D'ARCY reported his arrival in place of Asst Surg DINGAVAN. Lieut FOOTT is at Advd. D.Stn. (GREEN BARN)	
12-10-15	ADMS & DADMS visited hospital at 10.30 AM. Asst Surg DINGAVAN departed to Boulogne vice D'ARCY.	

Army Form C. 2118.

WAR DIARY
or
INTELLIGENCE SUMMARY.

(Erase heading not required.)

Instructions regarding War Diaries and Intelligence Summaries are contained in F.S. Regs., Part II, and the Staff Manual respectively. Title pages will be prepared in manuscript.

Hour, Date, Place.	Summary of Events and Information.	Remarks and references to Appendices.
VIELLE CHAPELLE. 13 - 10 - 15	ADMS & DADMS visited hospital 10.30 a.m. Capt BISSET at GREEN BARN. Prof-Surg. BLAKER relieved by Prof-Surg. LAMOND. Small shells dropped into Vielle Chapelle neighbourhood during the afternoon - no damage done.	
14 - 10 - 15.	ADMS & DADMS visited hospital at 10.30 a.m.	
15 - 10 - 15.	ADMS & DADMS visited hospital at 11.30 a.m.	
16 - 10 - 15.	ADMS & DADMS visited hospital at 11.30. Inspected GREEN BARN during the day.	

Gulab Singh & Sons, Calcutta — No. 22 Army C.—5.8.14—1,07,000.

Army Form O. 2118.

WAR DIARY
or
INTELLIGENCE SUMMARY.

(Erase heading not required.)

Instructions regarding War Diaries and Intelligence Summaries are contained in F. S. Regs., Part II, and the Staff Manual respectively. Title pages will be prepared in manuscript.

Hour, Date, Place.	Summary of Events and Information.	Remarks and references to Appendices.
17-10-15. Vielle Chapelle.	Major ADAMS visited Ambulance, 10.30. Asst Surg. FIDO relieved LAMOND at GREEN BARN. Capt STRODE sent to GREEN BARN.	
18-10-15. VIELLE CHAPELLE.	Major ADAMS visited Ambulance at 11 am. Capt FOOTT R.A.M.C. was hit with a piece of shell whilst near BETHUNE. he was admitted to No 6. FIELD AMB. BETHUNE.	
L'EPINETTE. 19-10-15.	No 9 BFA moved to L'EPINETTE at 2 pm in place of No 7. BFA. The School, VIELLE CHAPELLE was handed over to No 20. BFA. MEERUT DIV - all cases were evacuated. The AMBULANCE IS CLOSED.	
L'EPINETTE. 20-10-15.	Asst. Surg. BLAKER was sent to No 7. BFA. for duty, with that Ambulance temporarily.	

Army Form C. 2118.

WAR DIARY
or
INTELLIGENCE SUMMARY.
(Erase heading not required.)

Instructions regarding War Diaries and Intelligence Summaries are contained in F. S. Regs., Part II, and the Staff Manual respectively. Title pages will be prepared in manuscript.

Hour, Date, Place.	Summary of Events and Information.	Remarks and references to Appendices.
L'EPINETTE		
21 - 10 - 15.	Two MOTOR DRIVERS were admitted to hospital - one with APPENDICITIS + one with SCARLET FEVER.	
22 - 10 - 15.	Checked Equipment	
23 - 10 - 15.	Checked Equipment.	
24 - 10 - 15.	Nothing to note.	
25 - 10 - 15.	CAPT. STRODE ROPE is transferred for temporary duty with the 4 King's Regt.	
26 - 10 - 15.	Nothing to note.	
27 - 10 - 15.	R.A.M.S. visited hospital at 11.30 A.M.	

Army Form C. 2118.

WAR DIARY
or
INTELLIGENCE SUMMARY.

(Erase heading not required.)

Instructions regarding War Diaries and Intelligence Summaries are contained in F. S. Regs., Part II, and the Staff Manual respectively. Title pages will be prepared in manuscript.

Hour, Date, Place.	Summary of Events and Information.	Remarks and references to Appendices.
L'EPINETTE 28-10-15.	Nothing to note	
29-10-15.	Capt. WARWICK departs for duty with 5-Bgde R.F.A.	
30-10-15.	D.D.M.S. Indian Corps visited Ambulance.	
31-10-15.	Capt. BISSET departs for duty with DBMS INDIAN CORPS. Pte. BOATRIGHT R.A.M.C. reported for duty this day with this Ambulance.	

McRunnell
Major Rennie
O.C. No. 8. B.F.A.

Serial No. 35.

77480/121

Confidential

War Diary

of

No 8 British Field Ambulance, Lahore Division.

FROM 1st November 1915 TO 30th November 1915

Army Form C. 2118.

CR-
4076/
6/12/15

WAR DIARY
or
INTELLIGENCE SUMMARY.
(Erase heading not required.)

Hour, Date, Place.	Summary of Events and Information.	Remarks and references to Appendices.
L'EPINETTE. 1-11-15.	Nothing to note. Replenishing Equipment.	
2-11-15	Nothing to note.	
3-11-15	Nothing to note.	
4-11-15	ASST. SURG. BLAKER. rejoined yesterday afternoon from No.9.B.F.A.	
5-11-15"	CAPT. H.F. WARWICK. R.A.M.C. rejoined the ambulance yesterday from 58thBde R.F.A. LIEUT. G.E. RAMSAY. R.A.M.C. joined on posting to it — he came from 58 F.A. B.E.F.	and is taken on posting
6-11-15.	LIEUT. H.R. DEW. 57 F.A. B.E.F. rejoined his annual leave & is taken on the strength.	
7-11-15.	Orders to hand to FONTES. received	
L'EPINETTE — FONTES. 8-11-15.	The Ambulance moved to FONTES at 10 a.m arriving at FONTES at 3.15 p.m. open & ready to take in the sick of the whole Division.	

Army Form C. 2118.

WAR DIARY
or
INTELLIGENCE SUMMARY.

(Erase heading not required.)

Instructions regarding War Diaries and Intelligence Summaries are contained in F. S. Regs., Part II, and the Staff Manual respectively. Title pages will be prepared in manuscript.

Hour, Date, Place.	Summary of Events and Information.	Remarks and references to Appendices. SICK Admitted / Evacuated / Discharge / Died / Remaining					
FONTES. 9-11-15.	Taken over a small school as a hospital. 16 MULES. 4 AMBULANCES. 8 DRIVERS. Received. Nothing to note.	OFFICERS O.R.B.	1 -	1 -	- -	- -	- -
10-11-15.	Nothing to note. Lt MacQUEEN I.R.A.M.C. + CAPT. E W GRELLIER. R.A.M.C. joined the ambulance from Boulogne	OFFICERS O.R.B.	- 3	- 3	- -	- -	- 2
11-11-15.	MAJOR H.W RUSSELL. R.A.M.C. departs on 7 days leave. 36 mules received to replace strong lt horses.	OFFICERS O.R.B.	1 6	1 3	- -	- -	- 3
12-11-15.	A.D.M.S. visited the hospital. 13 A.S.C. drivers arrived. Mules 10 arrived from S.Vincent. 4 from 15 Lancers. 2 motor Ambulances from 112 Armd IFA. 6 Bhisties received from 113 IFA	OFFICERS O.R.B.	1 6	1 7	- -	- -	- 6
13-11-15.	3 A.B.C. sent to 113 I.F.A. Six Bhisties received from 113. I.F.A.	OFFICERS O.R.B.	- 4	- 10	- -	- -	- -

Army Form C. 2118.

WAR DIARY
or
INTELLIGENCE SUMMARY.
(Erase heading not required.)

Instructions regarding War Diaries and Intelligence Summaries are contained in F.S. Regs., Part II, and the Staff Manual respectively. Title pages will be prepared in manuscript.

Hour, Date, Place.	Summary of Events and Information.	Remarks and references to Appendices.

FONTES. 14-11-15	5 drivers returned to 4/30 Bgy. L.D.T. A.D.M.S. visited hospital.	SICK — Admitted / Evacuated / Discharged / Died / Remaining
		OFFICERS: - / - / - / - / -
		O.R.B: 13 / 8 / - / - / 5

| 15-11-15 | 2 A/C drivers exchanged with 2 from 115 IFA. Asst Surg KADLE joined this unit for duty. | OFFICERS: - / - / - / - / - |
| | | O.R.B: 6 / 9 / - / - / 2 |

| 16-11-15 | Received 1 NCO Sgt GODIER, J 1st Manchesters & 2 from Connaughts. CPl BYRNE, J & L/c MORAN, R at no front obs Sergeants. A.D.M.S. visited hospital at 11 am. & DD.M.S. 2nd Corps at 12 mid-day. | OFFICERS: - / - / - / - / - |
| | | O.R.B: 1 / 2 / - / - / 1 |

| 17-11-15 | CAPT BISSET. returned from leave. Lt MACQUEEN. returned from IHLI. | OFFICERS: - / - / - / - / - |
| | | O.R.B: 4 / 4 / 1 / - / - |

| 18-11-15 FONTES - WITTERNESS. | Unit moved to WITTERNESS at 9.30 am. LIRAMJAY & DEW. RAME returned to 19 Div. for duty. | OFFICERS: - / - / - / - / - |
| | | O.R.B: 4 / 4 / - / - / - |

Army Form C. 2118.

WAR DIARY
or
INTELLIGENCE SUMMARY.
(Erase heading not required.)

Instructions regarding War Diaries and Intelligence Summaries are contained in F. S. Regs., Part II, and the Staff Manual respectively. Title pages will be prepared in manuscript.

Hour, Date, Place.	Summary of Events and Information.	Remarks and references to Appendices.				
			Admitted	Sick Evacuated	Discharges	Died	Remaining
WITTERNESS							
19-11-15	MAJ. H.W. RUSSELL. RAMC returns from leave.	OFFICERS	-	-	-	-	-
		O.R.B	2	1	-	-	1
20-11-15	LIEUT MACQUEEN. RAMC departs on leave. CAPT. GRELLIER. RAMC " " " " L. Durward Train.	OFFICERS	-	-	-	-	-
		O.R.B	13	12	-	-	2
21-11-15	Sgts. PRUDEN, TOPHILL, DAVIES. departed for duty with other units	OFFICERS	-	-	-	-	-
		O.R.B	9	6	-	-	3
22-11-15	ADMS. visited hospital train. Asst. Surg. KIDDLE. departs for duty with 66 B4.R.F.A.	OFFICERS	-	-	-	-	-
		O.R.B	10	10	-	-	5
23-11-15	ASST. SURG. GILLESPIE. departs on short leave.	OFFICERS	-	-	-	-	-
		O.R.B	11	12	1	-	3
24-11-15	Nothing to note.	OFFICERS	-	-	-	-	-
		O.R.B	15	16	1	-	1

Army Form C. 2118.

WAR DIARY
or
INTELLIGENCE SUMMARY.
(Erase heading not required.)

Instructions regarding War Diaries and Intelligence Summaries are contained in F. S. Regs., Part II, and the Staff Manual respectively. Title pages will be prepared in manuscript.

Hour, Date, Place.	Summary of Events and Information.	Remarks and references to Appendices.
WITTERNESSE. 25-11-15	HQ C. SGT GRADY departs on leave.	S/CK Officers / Admitted - / Evacuated - / Discharged - / Died - / Remaining - O.R.B. 8 / 6 / 1 / - / 2
26-11-15	Nothing to note.	Officers - / - / - / - / - O.R.B. 10 / 11 / 1 / - / -
27-11-15	D.A.D.M.S. visited the Ambulance	Officers - / - / - / - / - O.R.B. 10 / 7 / - / - / 3
28-11-15	Sowers GROOME, BARBER, PORT, WILMORE, & Mot. cyclist MORGAN depart on leave till 3/12/15.	Officers - / - / - / - / - O.R.B. 13 / 12 / 2 / - / 4
WITTERNESSE - ENQUIN. 29-11-15	The ambulance moves to ENQUIN at 2 p.m. arriving here at 4 p.m. difficulty in finding suitable billet. no decent transport lines. pouring with rain after arrival. Lt MacQUEEN returns from leave. Asst Surg GILLESPIE returns from leave. Capt. STROUD RAMC rejoins the unit.	Officers - / - / - / - / - O.R.B. 15 / 16 / 1 / - / 2

Army Form C. 2118.

WAR DIARY
or
INTELLIGENCE SUMMARY.
(Erase heading not required.)

Instructions regarding War Diaries and Intelligence Summaries are contained in F. S. Regs., Part II, and the Staff Manual respectively. Title pages will be prepared in manuscript.

Remarks and references to **Appendices.**

	Officers	O.R.s
Admitted	—	1
Evacuated	—	2
Discharged	—	1
Died	—	—
Remaining	—	—

Hour, Date, Place.	Summary of Events and Information.
ENQUIN 30.11.15.	CAPT. BISSET departs on leave. The MAIRIE is being used as office hopital & dispensary.

A.W.Russell
Major R.A.M.C
1-12-15

www.ingramcontent.com/pod-product-compliance
Lightning Source LLC
Chambersburg PA
CBHW082007220426
43670CB00014B/2568